"You move me . . ."
—CHAIRMAN MAO, ADDRESSING THE PEOPLE'S LIBERATION ARMY

PRAISE FOR *THE LITTLE RED BOOK* OF ADOBE LIVEMOTION

"... the only original software guide, ever! With Derek as your comrade, you'll learn everything you need to know to get started with Live Motion—that is, if you don't die laughing. I can only hope that this is the first of many software guides by Derek Pell."

—Jon Warren Lentz, founder of Flash-Guru.com
and bestselling author of the *Flash 5 Bible*

"A fun and wild read ... Pell loads every page with hilarious and bizarre gags (like the Great Wall Mart and the Zedong Institute of Technology, or ZIT), cartoons and tall tales. ... he walks the first-time user through a step-by-step process to create better Web-pages with animation, sound and sexier banner ads."

—Peter Delevett, *San Jose Mercury News*

"Derek Pell is America's funniest writer. While reading *The Little Red Book of Adobe LiveMotion*, I found myself continuously laughing out loud. ... [this book] taught me everything I could ever imagine wanting to know about Flash animation. The best combination since pizza and beer!"

—Larry McCaffery, editor of *Storming the
Reality Studio and After Yesterday's Crash*

THE LITTLE RED BOOK
of
ADOBE LIVEMOTION

A Radical Guide to Flash Animation

DEREK PELL

No Starch Press, Inc.

San Francisco

The Little Red Book of Adobe LiveMotion © 2001 by Derek Pell.

Printed in the United States of America

1 2 3 4 5 6 7 8 9 10—04 03 02 01

Trademarked names are used throughout this book. Rather than use a trademark symbol with every occurrence of a trademarked name, we are using the names only in an editorial fashion and to the benefit of the trademark owner, with no intention of infringement of the trademark.

Publisher: William Pollock
Project Editor: Karol Jurado
Assistant Editor: Nick Hoff
Technical Reviewer: Lin Biao
Cover Design: Derek Pell
Interior Design: Octopod Studios
Composition: Magnolia Studio
Copyeditor: Rebecca Pepper
Proofreader: Elisabeth Beller
Indexer: Nancy Humphreys

Distributed to the book trade in the United States by Publishers Group West, 1700 Fourth St., Berkeley, CA 94710; phone: 800-788-3123; fax: 510-658-1834.

Distributed to the book trade in Canada by Jacqueline Gross & Associates, Inc., One Atlantic Ave., Suite 105, Toronto, Ontario M6K 3E7, Canada; phone: 416-531-6737; fax: 416-531-4259.

For information on translations or book distributors outside the United States, please contact No Starch Press directly:

No Starch Press
555 De Haro Street, Suite 250, San Francisco, CA 94107
phone: 415-863-9900; fax: 415-863-9950; info@nostarch.com; http://www.nostarch.com

Library of Congress Cataloging-in-Publication Data

Pell, Derek.
      The little red book of Adobe LiveMotion / Derek Pell.
           p. cm.
      Includes index.
      ISBN 1-886411-53-0 (pbk.)
      1. Computer animation. 2. Adobe LiveMotion. I. Title.

TR897.7 .P45 2001
006.6'96--dc21

                                        00-069104

ACKNOWLEDGMENTS

Deep gratitude goes to my family: my wife Sheila and son Nick, who weathered the storms of this book's creation; to my father, who supported the revolution well beyond the call of duty; to Donald and Marianne, for their support and sacrifices.

There were many friends and rebels who helped me complete my Long March, and they deserve special recognition. Without them, this book might still be just another communist plot. *Chris Councill (angel & wizard); Gary-Paul Prince (artist & Maoist matchmaker); Gaby, Marylaure & Michael (who made us feel at home in Virginia); Vince Bartolone, Miggs Burroughs, Peter Gambaccini, Hal Jaffe, Larry McCaffery, Jim McMenamin, and Jim Ricketts (RIP)—true comrades under fire.* They deserve all the italics.

The people at Adobe are a special breed. No wonder the company continues to rise like a shining red star. Joe Bowden (always there when I needed him), Michael Ninness (for his good cheer), and John "Little Elvis" Nack, for his fraternal wit in the thick of battle, and for steering this Helmsman in the right direction.

The No Starch troops were indispensable. Thanks to Karol Jurado, who kept the project going throughout the Cultural Revolution; to Nick Hoff and Rebecca Pepper, who tampered with my text and made it better; to Amanda Staab and Richard Meredith, fierce propagandists in the great struggle; and to Chairman Bill Pollock, for having the courage to take this leap into the unknown.

Finally, I dedicate this book to the memory of my mother. Her sense of humor brightened my world.

She once gave me a Mao button.

Derek Pell
Charlottesville, VA

BRIEF CONTENTS

CONTENTS IN DETAIL

1

BIRTH OF A FLASH-KILLER:
LiveMotion's Radical Roots and Rise to Power

2

ORGANIZE! ORGANIZE! ORGANIZE!

3

CAPITALIST TOOLS:
Working with the Toolbox, Vectors,
Palettes, and LiveMotion Objects

4

REVOLUTIONARY STYLES, TEXTURES, AND THE PEOPLE'S LIBERATION LIBRARY

5

TIMELINE BALLET:
Orchestrating the Motion Revolution

6

TEXTUAL MISCHIEF AND THE ART OF PROPAGANDA:
Animating Words and Text

7

MAO BUTTONS, GUERRILLA ROLLOVERS, AND MASS MOVEMENT:
Correct Behaviors and Interactive Elements

8

IMPORTING AND EXPORTING THE REVOLUTION:
Working with Layered Photoshop Files and Exporting Flash

9

THE PEOPLE'S WAR OF INDEPENDENTS:
Conquering Time-Independent Groups

10

THE GREAT WALL OF SOUND:
Adding Audio to Flash Animations

11

CAPITALIST FREELOADERS AND
PROLETARIAN PRELOADERS

12

THE CULT OF MOTION:
Building Great Socialist Web Sites

A

LONG MARCH SHORTCUTS, TIPS, AND TRICKS

B

MOTION RESOURCES ON THE WEB

Index
215

CULTURAL REVOLUTION, KITSCH, AND THE ORIGINS OF THIS ODD LITTLE BOOK

Many years ago, while living as a hippie in New York City, I happened upon a nondescript storefront and wandered inside.

China Books & Periodicals turned out to be a store unlike any I had ever seen. On the walls hung brightly colored Red Chinese propaganda posters, screaming *Revolution!* Chairman Mao Zedong—wart and all—was everywhere, hovering like a bloated float in the Macy's parade. He beamed down on bright-eyed Socialist workers and bushy-tailed Red Guards, who saluted him by waving copies of his best-selling book of quotations, informally known as *The Little Red Book.*

I was transfixed by the art and the aura, bright colors, erotic swirls of calligraphy—the bizarre marriage of political diatribe and beatific imagery. Confronted by an army of subversive books and broadsides, I ogled the budget pamphlets and zines from Communist China. Uniquely bound and sized, many had been printed on odoriferous handmade papers. The queer texts were badly translated for foreign consumption, with type that fairly

The Chairman displays LiveMotion prototype.

Original edition of The Little Red Book.

shrieked from the shelves. Titles flew out at me like outlandishly surreal insults aimed at enemies within and without. The glory of Maoism was trumpeted with blasts of discordant hyperbole. *Oppose Book Worship! . . . Follow the Liberation of Women in Albania! . . . Defeat Running Dog Imperialists and Their Lackeys! . . . The Secrets of Treating Deaf & Dumb Mutes . . . ?*

The latter volume had a particularly weird cover: an illustration of a soldier armed with an acupuncture needle, poised and resolute, about to pierce his own ear with the needle!

Yes, I bought it, and asked the clerk to wrap it in a plain brown paper bag. I knew I was on dangerous ground. Of course, my interests were entirely aesthetic, not political. Surely *my* government would understand...

After discovering this literary goldmine, I began haunting New York's Chinatown, the herb shops, pharmacies, and haberdasheries, where I bought funny-smelling toothpaste, plastic toys, and cans of who-knew-what. I then returned to my apartment to gawk at the packaging designs, study the labels, and drool over the sheer *coolness* of the stuff.

I grew dizzy with dreams of satirical art.

In that charged, fetishistic atmosphere, my artistic sensibility began to take form.

I went on to publish books, illustrated with my own handmade collages. Under the name Norman Conquest, I founded the international anticensorship art collective Beuyscouts of Amerika and created nearly 100 mixed-media book objects (see *Little Red Book with Hook* in the People's Gallery color section) and artworks in "multiple" editions. However, it wasn't until the late 1980s that I discovered computers and—most importantly—Adobe Photoshop. It was then that I packed away for good my razors, scissors, and spray adhesive.

When I discovered the Web, I was immediately struck with the desire to animate—GIFs, of course, for there was no such thing as Flash back then. Today, however, you can export GIF and Flash animations with Adobe LiveMotion. While I use and admire Macromedia Flash,[1] the authoring program remains difficult to master and far from intuitive. Since I'm not a programmer and have neither the patience nor aptitude for writing code, I spend most of my time in Adobe LiveMotion. It lets me design interactive pages, layouts, navigation buttons, and JavaScript rollovers with ease.

It is truly a Web graphics package for the Masses.

Please Don't Squeeze the Chairman

What, I wonder, would Mao say about this rip-off of his book and image? Undoubtedly I'd be labeled a *zalan goutou xiao pachong da pashou wangba gaozi!*[2]—or worse. I'd be put on trial as one of the Gang of Five.

---

[1] All jokes aimed at Macromedia are intended as good clean fun. Like Adobe, Macromedia's products are awesome achievements. I'd certainly hate to have to build a Web site without Dreamweaver.

[2] Rotten dog's head, little reptile big pickpocket, cuckold kid!

But it hardly matters now that the Chairman has become an omnipotent pop icon, a grand Pooh-bah, a capitalist tool appropriated to sell everything from cornflakes to personal hygiene (see the People's Gallery color insert section). Yes, the Chairman is probably spinning in his grave, and wouldn't that make a great Flash animation!

Infamous PAA propaganda poster (Anonymous, 2000).

But, you may ask, is it proper, that is, *correct* Marxist–Leninist–Mao Zedong Thought to publish a computer book filled with satire, puns, and visual mischief?

Of course it is—especially when the goal is to revolutionize the computer book industry by defeating all big fat feudalist manuals and replacing them with svelte, absurdist guides bent on Web domination.

And as the Web continues to evolve and revolutionize our lives, I think it's fitting that I resurrect the obese ghost of Mao Zedong to spur us on to bolder experiments, so that we may create great and glorious images and engaging, immersive, interactive animations for the Web.

Web Workers of the World, Unite!

The Chairman displays a LiveMotion prototype.

1

BIRTH OF A FLASH-KILLER:
LiveMotion's Radical Roots
and Rise to Power

In January of 1999, deep in the digital jungles of Silicon Valley, a revolution was brewing. A radical band of software developers gathered in secrecy and hatched a plot to create a weapon that could overthrow Macromedia Flash. Although the Flash animation format (.swf) was well on its way toward Web domination, the Flash authoring environment was vulnerable to attack. The conspirators were determined to defeat the upstart forces of Macromedia. Not only was the Flash program's interface as forbidding as a bust of Mao, but its frame-based Timeline (the rebels called it the "frameline") was largely an artifact of Flash's birth as a cartooning tool. "A user-snoozer," one comrade cracked. The new weapon would employ the simplicity and elegance of the timeline found in Adobe's video editing software, AfterEffects. The thinking was this: If you can animate only one object per layer (as in Flash), why not have the layers be equal objects? That way everything can be animated![1]

The rebels (we'll call them the Adobe Motion Patrol) found additional seeds for their secret weapon embedded in ImageStyler (see Figure 1-1), an earlier (1998) Adobe Web graphics product

---

[1] "Thoroughly smash the old animation path!" —Mao Zedong

Figure 1-1: Revolutionary precursor: Adobe ImageStyler.

that enjoyed a cult status among the People. If the new product could build on the powerful foundation of ImageStyler and be given an intuitive timeline such as the one in AfterEffects, the world would rejoice and embrace The Great Animation Revolution with Adobean Characteristics!

The Shot Heard 'Round the Web

On March 6, 2000, in San Jose, California, Adobe Systems' Motion Patrol launched its sneak attack, proudly proclaiming the release of a new public beta: LiveMotion. The Revolution was afoot!

Here was a fierce arsenal of animation tools, a dynamic Web graphics package that combined vector-based drawing and shape tools with advanced raster gear in a single incendiary package. Hordes of dispossessed Motion Cadres greeted the smiling (and familiar) Adobe interface with cheers. At the heart of this new Web-volutionary weapon was its tight integration with other popular Adobe products and the awesome ability to import Photoshop and Illustrator files. Each layer was easily transformed into separate objects ready for manipulation, and every object's attributes could be independently animated right on the Timeline! (You'll learn more about attributes in Chapter 5.)

Why, a dedicated follower could even apply Photoshop filters from within the belly of the beast or drag and drop bitmaps and sound files and export to a variety of formats.

And talk about radical chic—multiple effects applied to an object could be saved as a reusable style. All objects remained editable (*nondestructive* in Adobe-speak) throughout the design process; thus, wrong-headed, anti-Maoist design ideas could be easily purged and replaced with new ones.[2]

LiveMotion even came loaded with a powerful *auto-tweening* feature for automatically inserting animation frames between defined keyframes, thus dramatically reducing the imperialist lackey slave labor required to produce smooth Flash animations. At long last, the codeless masses were free to create their own motion graphics!

Word of the new weapon spread like wildfire though cyberspace, igniting the imagination of rebel artists and designers around the globe, inciting downtrodden geeks and weary workers to rise up and cheer the New People's Interface (NPI). A better Mao's trap had arrived, and the ranks of the People's Animation Army swelled. The beta was quickly branded a "Flash-killer"[3] by the People.

Dot-Commies in Cyberspace

If there were any doubts as to the revolutionary nature of Live-Motion, the version 1.0 package should dispel them. On the product box and CD label (and even atop the program's omnipresent toolbar) is a red and yellow futuristic Chinese fighter jet, manned by a little Red pilot.[4]

Figure 1-2: An undocumented Easter egg.

---

[2] Mao Zedong Motion Thought is the crystallization of collective design wisdom.
[3] The high command at Adobe officially disavows this term, believing that LiveMotion 1.0 was a shot across the bow, not the coup de grace.
[4] Modeled after ace pilot Wang "Hotdog" Wei.

It is even rumored that the program contains a subversive Easter egg—a QuickTime movie featuring Mao and Richard Nixon (see Figure 1-2)—although I've yet to establish its origin.

Is LiveMotion for Me?

If you're a beginner eager to learn Web animation, LiveMotion is a great place to start and a great place to grow. Whereas Macromedia Flash requires considerable time and effort to learn its techniques, you can create a simple animation with LiveMotion in minutes since the software does most of the work for you. Dig deeper and you'll see that it's capable of producing state-of-the-art motion graphics. And if you're a Maoist . . . well, what the hell else are you going to buy?

Is This Little Red Book for Me?

This Little Red Book will not teach you everything, but it will teach you a lot about LiveMotion—like how to produce cool Flash animations and uncompromising layouts; how to use vector shape-creation tools, styles, behaviors; and how to make preloaders, rollovers, and Mao buttons! As you've already seen, this book is not only different from the other books on LiveMotion—it's unlike any computer book ever written. At the very least, consider it an investment, as it's sure to become a collector's item.

It'll make you laugh out loud—right in the middle of a technical exercise. It'll jump out and goose you. If that's a distraction, then purchase a different book. If you like satire and surprises, buy this one.

It gets a little weird in places, too. It has dark moments you won't find in those dime-a-dozen dummies books. It has outrageous art unseen in technical books that will up your vision and inspire you to break out of the box of stale Web design. And Mao—this book has more images of Mao than the Chinese Communist Party Archive.

Priceless porcelain pencil vase (author's collection).

In most cases, my animation examples here use a minimum number of objects. This should make it easier for you to follow them. It also happens to reflect my own personal "style" and approach to animation. Do not, however, infer from this that LiveMotion doesn't let you animate dozens of objects in complex, mysterious ways. Your creations will ultimately reflect whatever style and approach best suits *you*—the program will adapt to your dreams and desires.

What this book will *not* do is provide you with a dozen different ways to achieve the same task. I'll detail what I think is the easiest method for a certain task. One of my main complaints with a lot of computer books is that the text often becomes so cluttered with directions it's impossible to read.

Since at the moment, LiveMotion is only in version 1.0.2, it has its quirks, quicksand, and omissions. And speaking of omissions: The *Adobe LiveMotion User Guide* is not only poorly bound (after one use the pages fall out)[5], but it leaves plenty to the imagination. For example, one of the hottest topics on the LiveMotion forums is how to build a preloader—yet the *User Guide* doesn't even mention preloaders.

Together we'll move beyond these deficiencies to unleash the power of the fiery red dragon inside. In the pages that follow, you'll find helpful hints, tricks, White Bone Demons, and undocumented secrets that will enable you to get more out of the software. Unlike other computer books, this one was designed to be red and *read*.

What You Need to Get the Most from This Book

This book assumes a basic familiarity with Photoshop. Today, nearly every image you see in print or on the Web has been touched by it, if not created with it from scratch. I've yet to find a professional who doesn't use it, yet it's accessible to beginners so long as the desire is there. If you don't own it, beg, borrow, or steal to get it. It can throw open dozens of digital doors and has the power to change your life as an artist. Besides, Photoshop and LiveMotion are comrades-in-arms; they work together seamlessly to create revolutionary graphics.

In addition to LiveMotion, Photoshop, and plenty of snacks, what equipment do you need? Well, a computer might be nice—with as much RAM as your budget will bear. Although not essential, a large monitor is helpful when navigating the program's Timeline, which can stretch from here to China.

---

[5] I recommend leaving the *User Guide* in its shrink-wrap. Stash it away in a safe place, for it will one day be worth a fortune—just like the Chinese pencil vase I own, featuring Mao with his would-be assassin, Lin Biao.

Beware the White Bone Demon

Propaganda aside, LiveMotion has its shortcomings and quirks, so this book includes plenty of tricks, tips, and workarounds to help you over the bumps and land mines.

Be sure to watch for the White Bone Demon[6] symbol (Figure 1-3) used throughout the book. These sidebars contain undocumented tips and advice on what to do when bitten by bugs.

Figure 1-3: Beware of White Bone Demons.

Finally, surf on over to my companion Web site at www.littleredbooks.com. It features LiveMotion samples, additional resources, live links, and Maoist art deemed too radical for this book. Also, look carefully and you'll find some *free* (collectable) Little Red Book goodies.

Publisher's Note: Possession of this book in international airports or while crossing state lines may result in unusual delays. The publisher assumes no responsibility for any such delays or inconveniences.

---

[6] Jiang Qing; Mao Zedong's fourth wife. Jiang (aka Shrew Manchu), a third-rate actress who starred in the capitalist roader production of *For Whom the Bone Tolls*, was best known for henpecking the Chairman throughout the Great Cultural Revolution.

The Chairman says, "Never gather forces in the middle of a battle."

2

ORGANIZE!
ORGANIZE!
ORGANIZE!

Well, he didn't actually say that, but he could have. You don't want to get caught in the middle of an animation and have to break your momentum to start foraging for files. All dedicated Flash cadets know that Discipline is the key to success, and "Organize!" is our battle cry.

Web brigades are often ordered to create complex, interactive animations, combining many elements (vector shapes, photographs, JavaScript rollovers, audio clips, and so on). These assignments are often accompanied by impossible deadlines:

"The Chairman needs to see the finished project yesterday!"

This translates into extra trips to Little Red Starbucks (see Figure 2-1) to reload Java mugs, lots of pressure, and maybe a few all-nighters. We rarely have the luxury of spending a month or two in development. Instead, we slave away at our workstations, keeping one bloodshot eye on the clock. But we can minimize our stress and let, if not a hundred, at least a couple of flowers bloom in the Red Sun by organizing effectively.

Figure 2-1: Little Red Starbucks.

Conspire, Plot, Plan Ahead!

Organization is essential to building successful Web designs and motion graphics, not to mention revolutions. Even with less complex projects, you'll find that it pays to plan ahead.

You'll conserve energy and save yourself countless hours if you map out your creations in advance. As obvious as it may sound, people plunge ahead without a strategy and wind up with lifeless or confusing Flash-in-the-pans. Oppose the cowshed Web mess with Correct Mao Zedong Principles of Preparation!

The following is my approach to organization. It's fully customizable and without contradictions. Adapt it to suit your needs.

Motion Notions

First, appropriate a pencil and notebook (a red one is highly recommended) and write down your ideas for the animation. Include a list of assets you plan to use. Map out as much of the project as possible, including any unusual fonts and effects you want to employ. Make thumbnails and sketch out each scene (see Figure 2-2). The latter is a great aid to the creative process, giving you a script to work from. I like to think of every LiveMotion animation as a mini-movie, with a beginning, middle, and victorious end. And if donning an ascot or using a cigarette holder helps—do it. As the Chairman would say, the ends justify the means.

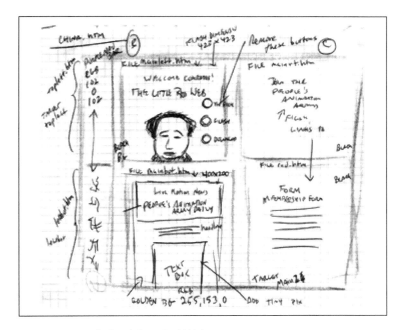

Figure 2-2: Rough sketch for a Red Web page.

After you've hatched your plan of attack, create a project folder on your desktop (see Figure 2-3) and make a series of subfolders inside this folder, for example: Notes, Originals, Vectors, Bitmaps, Flash, and Audio.

Once you've created and assembled your files (that is, clipart or your own original graphics), you can drag and drop them into their respective folders.

Red Guard Those Files!

Making backups may not be a revolutionary concept, but it can definitely save your backside. Whether it's manually copying files to a floppy or Zip disk or automating the process and backing up to a tape drive or CD-RW, a backup strategy is critical. (See the discussion of the program Second Copy later in this chapter.) Preserve all of your original LiveMotion files (.liv) even after you've exported them to other formats (such as .gif, .swf, or .html). That way you can always go back and update them as needed. No sense having to reinvent the Great Wall.

Figure 2-3: Sample desktop organized for battle.

Revolutionary Tools and Digital Comrades

As wonderful as LiveMotion is, it becomes even more powerful when used in concert with other revolutionary tools. Remember, animation power grows out of the barrels of many guns.

The Big Guns

Access to Adobe Photoshop is essential. It's arguably the most influential graphics software ever created, and nearly all of the printed and Web-based images surrounding us have, in part, been created or enhanced by it. Since both Photoshop and Adobe Illustrator work hand-in-glove with LiveMotion, they are must-haves. (In Chapter 8, you'll see how you can drag and drop layered files from these programs right into your LiveMotion composition to create animations.)

At the risk of being branded a "feudalist gangster element," I confess I don't use Adobe GoLive to build my Web pages. Macromedia's Dreamweaver 4 is my weapon of choice—it's packed with power and, in my opinion, more intuitive than GoLive. Those who appreciated the simplicity and design of Adobe PageMill will love Dreamweaver. It handles LiveMotion's exported HTML and Flash files flawlessly.

The Little Guns

Here are a few little Red Guardians that should be in every revolutionary's bag of chop-tricks:

- **Second Copy.** This elegant, easy-to-use program was *Dingbat Magazine*'s Best Utility of 1999 and is still going strong. It takes all the fuss and worry out of backing up your vital files. (Centered Systems, www.centered.com)
- **Cool Ruler.** When you need a quick, precise measurement (pixels, centimeters, or inches), just click to bring up this nifty stay-on-top ruler. It even has a built-in calculator and—in the spirit of Mao—it's *free*! (FabSoft, www.fabsoft.com)
- **Csamp.** Another liberated freebie, Csamp lets you sample colors from any open window or object on your desktop and gives you RGB values that you can then copy to the Clipboard. (DV Labs, home.talkcity.com/ComputerCt/vdamjan/)
- **Swish.** This is the first program to simplify stunning Flash-based text effects. You can apply these effects to images, too. What would take hours to accomplish in LiveMotion or Flash can be done in a matter of minutes with Swish. Although you can't directly place or import .swf files into LiveMotion, you can access them by appending them to your movies (see Chapter 9). (Swish, www.swishzone.com)
- **SWfx.** Click and apply 100 complex animated text effects. It's like Swish on steroids. (Wildform, www.wildform.com)
- **SoundForge.** Mix, edit, and convert your own audio files for use in LiveMotion. Lets you orchestrate and collage those raw sounds into smooth soundtracks. (Sonic Foundry, www.sonicfoundry.com)

Now that you've got your comrades assembled, you're ready to fire up LiveMotion and blast the Ruling Class.

"Don't underestimate the Capitalists . . . . They know their tools."

3

CAPITALIST TOOLS:
Working with the Toolbox,
Vectors, Palettes, and
LiveMotion Objects

LiveMotion's interface is as friendly and beatific as Mao's smiling face (without the bloat). One glance at the Toolbox (see Figure 3-1) and you'll see you're not in enemy territory. In fact, you'll probably think you've launched Photoshop by mistake (see Figure 3-2). Just look at the familiar icons: Type tool, Crop tool, Paint Bucket, Hand tool, Pen, Eyedropper, Zoom. (Repeat three times aloud—it's poetry!)

All Right-Thinking Little Red Guards Should Look Alike!

Adobe's consistent user interface is a blessing for us lowly Web workers: It crushingly defeats the dreaded SLC (steep learning curve) like a paltry Paper Tiger.

You will learn to cherish LiveMotion's unique object layer system. It's dramatically different from Photoshop's document layers and uses an *object-based* editing model; that is, each object in a composition is independent and can be composed of multiple layers. Object-based editing is especially useful for creating drop shadows and manipulating textures.

The Toolbox

At the top of the Toolbox (Figure 3-1), to the right of the crucial Selection arrow, is a white arrow with a tiny plus sign. This is the Subgroup[1] Selection tool for selecting groups of objects or objects within groups. Below it are the Drag Selection (the white arrow with the dotted box) and Layer Offset (the white layers with the double arrow) tools. The former lets you grab objects hidden behind other objects, and the latter moves selected layers.

Figure 3-1: LiveMotion Toolbox.

Figure 3-2: Photoshop Toolbox.

You're well armed with all of the basic vector drawing tools for making rectangles, rounded rectangles, ellipses, and polygons—Adobe leaves no shape unturned. However, the program supports

---

[1] Not to be confused with Subversive Group.

only stroke or fill on objects, not both at once. You can get around this limitation by duplicating an object and switching it from fill to stroke or vice versa. For example, here's one way to create a red square with a black outline:

1. Set your fill color to black by choosing it from the Color palette.

2. Using the Rectangle tool, drag to create a black rectangle of any size. (Note: Fill is the default setting in the Properties palette.)

3. Change the proportions of the object from the Transform palette. Double-click inside the little window displaying the object's width. Type 200 and press ENTER. Press TAB to jump to the height window and again type 200 and press ENTER.

4. Press CTRL-D to duplicate the black square. (LiveMotion places the duplicate directly on top of the original, so you won't see it. Take my word for it: It's there.)

5. The duplicate is automatically selected. Choose a nice bright shade of red from the Color palette.

6. Using the Transform palette in the manner described in Step 3, change the dimensions of the object to 185 x 185.

7. Pause to admire your Red Square with its bold black outline.

White Bone Demon

Beware of this simple fact, Comrades: Any object with more than one object layer will export to Flash as a bitmap. That means a fatter file. LiveMotion styles preserve layers, so if you apply a complex style to a shape, LiveMotion will add layers as necessary. A change to the shape of one layer will change the shape of the others, but layers can still have different colors, sizes, textures, positions, degrees of softness, and other settings.

Some objects (polygons) can be converted to other shapes (circles, rectangles, and so on) via the Properties palette. Most importantly, when you vary an object's shape and characteristics (number of sides, size, rotation, and so on), the visual style updates automatically. (See Chapter 4 for a detailed look at styles.)

The Type tool in LiveMotion is a bit more limited than the one in Photoshop: It can use only one font and size per text object, and it likes you to hard-wrap your text lines (that is, to use hard returns to make your text wrap), so you don't get the dreaded "Some objects were too large to render" error. On the bright side, the Type tool has some cool vertical text features (see Chapter 6), and nearly all of its attributes (including tracking) can be animated.

Don't be fooled by LiveMotion's Crop tool. Although it looks exactly like the one in Photoshop, it does not work in the same way. LiveMotion uses it to crop objects, *not* the composition.

At the bottom of the Toolbox are two squares showing the object fill and composition background color. Below it is a hand with upraised finger, which might suggest a stern Red Guard lecture on Party Discipline but in actuality launches Preview mode for viewing animations "live" inside LiveMotion. (Later on, you'll learn to preview your animations in a Web browser for maximum ideological fidelity.) The depressed button with the black arrow next to the Preview mode button indicates that you are in Edit mode.

Preferences and Proletarian Perks

Whether by oversight or plot, LiveMotion requires that you have a document open before you can edit the preferences. You'll find them under the Edit menu (Edit • Preferences). There are only a few choices, only one of which I recommend checking—Auto-Revert to Arrow tool. This option is quite helpful, as it automatically switches your crosshair cursor back to the Selection tool after you've used any other tool.

NOTE *If you choose not to set this preference, you can always press V on your keyboard to change the crosshair cursor back to the Selection arrow. In fact, holding down any tool selection key will temporarily toggle your tool to the one you're pressing. So, for example, if you want to use the Layer Offset tool briefly while using the Rectangle tool, just hold down the O key as you draw. See Chapter 12 for a complete list of hotkeys.*

Creating a New Composition

Selecting File • New creates a new composition and lets you choose your basic settings (see Figure 3-3). You can make changes in these settings at any time by selecting Edit • Composition Settings. Still, it's helpful to determine your dimensions in advance as resizing a composition in LiveMotion is not as efficient as changing the canvas size in Photoshop.

For most Flash animations, a frame rate of 10 or 12 frames per second (fps) should be sufficient to achieve smooth results. Bear in

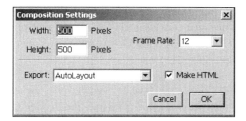

Figure 3-3: Composition settings.

mind that the higher the frame rate the bigger your final file size. Too low a setting makes for jerky, Charlie Chaplin–like effects.

One of LiveMotion's distinct advantages over Macromedia Flash is the fact that you can change your frame rate without changing the timing of your animation. In Flash, you are limited by its revisionist "frameline." For example, if your animation lasts 3 seconds at 10 fps, it'll last just 1 second at 30 fps. By contrast, in LiveMotion's revolutionary Timeline, the same animation will last the same 3 seconds, since the program automatically creates the necessary frames. (See Chapter 5 for a complete discussion of the great People's Timeline.)

Exporting Revolution

After you've created an animation in LiveMotion, you'll most likely want to export it as a Flash file (.swf). Although you can export GIF animations, this book will focus on the Flash format, since that's where LiveMotion shines as bright as the reddest Red Sun. (The parameters for exporting to Flash are covered in detail in Chapter 9.)

Other important avenues for exporting your compositions can be found in the Composition Settings dialog box (Edit • Composition Settings):

- **AutoLayout.** This is the default setting. It magically slices the composition, creates a table, and generates an HTML page that preserves your precious LiveMotion layout—WYSIWYG.

- **Entire Composition.** Exports the entire composition as a single image.

- **Trimmed Composition.** Turns the composition into a single image. However, it also trims the excess bourgeoisie fat; that is, it removes all the empty background space. This option can save you valuable bytes.

- **AutoSlice.** Exports each object or group of objects as individual files and creates an HTML file if you're exporting as a bitmap format (GIF, JPEG, and so on).

Strange Characters

Before we take a whirlwind tour of LiveMotion's palettes, let's get our hands dirty and have some fun with one of my favorite Capitalist tools—the mighty Pen! The Pen is the shining path to great revolutionary shapes, not to mention straight lines, curves, and corners.

Let's start by drawing a Chinese character. Don't worry, I'm not attempting to teach you Chinese, but what better way to start drawing than by using a Chinese pictogram? In addition to their raw, impressionistic beauty, Chinese characters can trigger the imagination—a creative Red Guard Rorschach test.

MAC PARTISANS *Refer to Appendix A, "Long March Shortcuts for the Mac," for politically correct keyboard combinations.*

We'll work with this character, which I scanned from an old Chinese woodcut:

Strange character.

What does it look like to you? If you answered "Imperialist running dog," you're a hardcore revolutionary—award yourself three red stars. If, however, you thought "jogger," you've flunked the quiz and will be sent to the Worker's Commune for some serious Self-Criticism. Remember, this is *my* Little Red Book and *I'm* the dictator.

Draw the Character

But back to the drawing. Seize character.gif from the People's Download Page at www.littleredbooks.com. If you're blessed with a good eye for detail, attempt to copy it by working alongside the original. If you're blessed with a true Eagle Eye, simply use the book's illustration. On the other hand, if you're an anarchist, feel free to create any crazy character you want.

By clicking with the Pen tool, you make control points with connecting lines. Control points set the beginning and end of each line and define a path. You can add control points along a path, convert corner points to smooth points, and draw Bezier curves by clicking the initial control point and dragging. We'll begin by drawing straight lines to make the basic shape, and then we'll smooth them.

1. Start a blank composition and size it at 500 pixels x 500 pixels. Press CTRL-S to save and name the file. Save your work frequently!

2. Select the Pen tool. Make sure Outline is checked in the Property palette (in the upper right corner of your screen), and set the line width to 2.

3. Click and create a series of control points approximating the shape of the character's "head." Close the shape by clicking on your starting control point. (Don't worry about precision; a rough look-alike is all we're after.) Figure 3-4 shows my version rendered with eight control points.

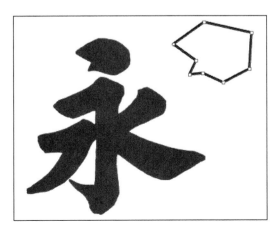

Figure 3-4: Connect the "Dot-Commies" and create the "head."

4. Draw the body in the same fashion as Step 3 (see Figure 3-5).

Figure 3-5: Head and body shape.

Smooth the Points

Now we'll smooth the corner points.

1. With the Pen tool selected, hold down the ALT key and position the crosshair cursor over any corner point you want to smooth. When the crosshair cursor becomes an arrow, click on the point (still holding down ALT). A small bar with two handles appears.

2. Drag the handles to adjust the line's curve. The handles will vanish as soon as you click on another control point. To adjust an object whose control points are hidden, approach a segment of the object with the Pen Selection tool, and when the crosshair cursor turns into an arrow, click the segment. The control points reappear.

> **NOTE** *The Pen Selection tool is essential for stretching and repositioning your line segments. To quickly switch between the Pen and the Pen Selection tool, hold down the CTRL key.*

Don't panic if you make a mistake; just press CTRL-Z to undo it. (LiveMotion supports 20 undos[2]—that's more than enough for even the most misguided Maoist.) You can delete a line segment by positioning the Pen over a corner point (a tiny minus sign will appear) and clicking.

3. Add control points by clicking anywhere on a line segment. Clicking on an existing point erases it.

When you're finished, the character should look something like my Imperialist Running Dog in Figure 3-6.

---

[2] Not to be confused with "the three red banners," "the fours olds," "the five-anti campaign," or the "ten years of turmoil."

If you placed the original character.gif as a guide, click to select it, and press ENTER to make it disappear.

Adjust the Object's Size and Color

If you're not happy with the object's size, click on the object to select it (its bounding box appears). You can then stretch and resize it by dragging one of the six solid handles surrounding the bound-

Figure 3-6: Working the angles.

ing box. To resize the object proportionally, you must hold down the SHIFT key while dragging.

The hollow handle in the upper right corner of the bounding box lets you rotate the object.

REVOLUTIONARY TRICKS *To rotate an object using the other corner handles, hold down ctrl-shift and then rotate. In general, holding down ctrl over a handle gives you the opposite of its standard function, pressing ctrl changes the upper right handle from rotation to scale, the other corners from scale to rotation, and the side handles from stretch to skew.)*

1. Using the Selection tool, position your mouse in the upper left corner of the composition, then click and drag diagonally to select both shapes.

2. Place your crosshair cursor anywhere on either object's line (not its bounding box!) until it becomes an arrow. Now click and drag to reposition the character in the center of the composition. (If your crosshair cursor didn't switch back to the main Selection arrow automatically, tap the letter V on your keyboard.)

3. From the menu bar, choose Object • Combine • Unite to join the two shapes into a single object.

4. In the Color palette, set the top slider all the way to the right to give the Imperialist Running Dog a thin red outline.

5. In the Properties palette, set the width slider to 19 for a nice bold appearance.

6. Select Fill to create a solid red Imperialist Running Dog just like the original figure. Save your file.

Add the Character to the Library

Now let's add the character to the Library so we can access it later.

1. Click the Library palette tab. Select the character, then drag and drop it into the Library.

2. A dialog box appears. Type a name ("Running Dog" or whatever you wish). Press ENTER to close the dialog box.

Now your character has a safe home in the heart of the People's Liberation Library. We'll discuss the Library in greater depth in Chapter 4.

More Pen Fun

Before moving on to discuss LiveMotion's basic palettes, let's explore the Pen tool further. We'll start with some curves: Draw a curved line with the Pen by clicking inside the composition to set a control point and start a line segment. Drag the mouse to set the depth of the curve. Curves are a bit tricky at first, but with a little practice you'll soon get a feel for them. Once you've used the Pen to make a shape, you can manipulate it endlessly.

NOTE *You can't immediately manipulate an object made with one of the shape tools (Rectangle, Ellipse, and so on). You must first turn it into a path.*

Armed with a new sense of freedom, let's subvert some party lines.

1. Start a new composition.

2. Draw an unfilled rounded rectangle, using the Rounded Rectangle tool.

3. Set the line width in the Properties palette to 4.

4. Change to the Selection tool (press the V key), and select the rectangle.

5. In the Properties palette, choose Path from the drop-down menu. Now the lines can be subverted to nefarious purpose. You can get the same effect by clicking the rectangle with the Pen Selection tool to reveal its control points. Once you do so, you won't be able to adjust some of the object's properties (in this case, the corner radius of the rounded rectangle).

6. With the Pen tool, add four control points, evenly spaced between the corners. Remember to position the Pen at the line's center until the small x becomes a +. You may have to maneuver the mouse a bit for the + to reveal itself—once it does, click the line.

7. Hold down CTRL to switch to the Pen Selection tool and, one at a time, select the points and drag each toward the object's center to form a star.

8. Choose Fill from the Properties palette and select a hue from the Color palette. Suggestion: Use Mao's favorite color.

Creating a Red Star is certainly fun, but let's get radical and drag all of the control points into a maze of angles. Pretend you're in the midst of the Cultural Revolution . . . . Let chaos reign: Select Fill from the Properties palette and try clicking the Pen randomly across the composition. You'll have instant abstract art (see Figure 3-7).

Figure 3-7: Character assassination.

With a little practice, you'll discover the power of Live-Motion's vector drawing tools. Whether it's a crude cartoon like my chicken man in Figure 3-8 (created with straight lines using only the Pen and Rounded Rectangle tools) or abstract shapes such as those in Figure 3-7, the methodical process of adding control points along a path, converting corners to curves, and tweaking and stretching line segments enables you to draw virtually anything you want.

Indeed, the Pen is mightier than the hand grenade.

Figure 3-8: Chicken man.

The People's Palettes

When you first launch LiveMotion, it blossoms forth with all its palettes stacked neatly on the right of your screen. Their innovative tabbed design keeps clutter to a minimum, allowing you to swap, arrange, or isolate the nested items by dragging the tabs to the desired position. After you've become comfortable with the program, you'll probably want to customize the default arrangement to suit your needs.

You can banish all of the palettes in one fell swoop by simply pressing SHIFT-TAB. Presto—the Toolbox remains visible, just as in Photoshop. Press SHIFT-TAB again, and the palettes reappear. You can also access them from the Window menu, or you can reset them to their original layout using the Reset to Defaults command on the Window menu.

Let's take a closer look at a few of the palettes to see what they have to offer.

The Properties Palette

With Zen-like simplicity, the Properties palette gives you the choice of having either a solid filled shape or an outline of any width you desire. Remember, when working in LiveMotion, you always begin with an *object*. Objects are the nascent source of revolutionary zeal—like the barefoot doctor or peasant who volunteers to serve the People in the PAA (People's Animation Army)—a raw recruit eager to be whipped into ideological shape. Then, through rigorous anti-feudal training, special effects, and Flashist fervor, the object-recruit is transformed into a shining example of Revolutionary Spirit—an animated Motion Cadre!

1. Start a new composition and leave the default settings in place.

2. From the Toolbox, select the Ellipse tool; click the Properties tab (Figure 3-9), and select Outline.

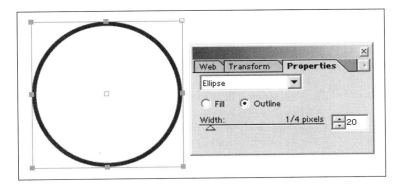

Figure 3-9: The Properties palette.

3. Using the slider bar, set the outline width to 20 pixels. Now hold down SHIFT and draw a circle (any size will do). The circle appears with a thick black outline.

4. Change the outline's color to red by selecting the Eyedropper tool and clicking on red in the Color palette's rainbow bar. (The arrow to the right of the Color tab provides a variety of views: Saturation, Value, Hue, RGB, and CIEL). Return to the Properties palette and select Fill for a solid red circle.

If you decide you'd rather have a rectangle instead, just click the arrow next to Ellipse and choose Rectangle from the list.

The Transform Palette

From the Transform palette, you can precisely position your object via the *X* and *Y* coordinates as well as rotate, stretch, or skew it. More often than not, you'll be moving your objects with the cross-hair cursor, but when precision is required, this is the palette to use.

NOTE *For layouts, you'll want to use the grids and rulers found under the View menu. (You can specify precise grid spacing from Preferences (Edit • Preferences).*

The Opacity Palette

You can change the opacity of your little red rectangle from the Opacity palette. You can also give it a variety of gradient fills.

These effects are applied to either an object's fill or its outline, depending on what property is selected. Controlling an object's opacity holds the key to powerful animations and rollover effects. You'll learn how to do this later in the book.

The 3D Palette

The 3D palette lets you quickly transform a rectangle into a bare bones button for the Web. (Chapter 7 talks about the Rollovers palette and shows how the 3D palette makes the task of creating a convincing button easier than debunking the lies of a fatuous counterrevolutionary.)

To make a button, go to the 3D tab and select Emboss from the drop-down menu. Set the desired Depth, Softness, and Lighting via the slider bars. For more radical results, toy with the Ripple effect (located in the Edge drop-down menu) by tweaking the Depth slider. Also try experimenting with the various Edge and Light effects.

Trial and error produced the cool radar screen effect in Figure 3-10.

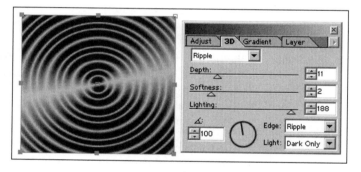

Figure 3-10: Just a blip on the radar screen.

Behind the humble façade of the People's Palettes lie powerful controls capable of creating Victorious Layouts and Advanced Motion Graphics. Explore them deeply, Comrades, for they offer rewards that are truly revolutionary.

Working with Objects

Imagine yourself a student at Zedong Institute of Technology (ZIT). There are no teachers; they have all been banished to labor camps for reeducation and Socialist Animation Training (SAT). The classrooms are filled with brightly colored Big Character

Posters denouncing U.S. politicians—**DOWN WITH SON OF A BUSH!**—and extolling the teachings of pinko satirists—**OPPOSE BOOK WORSHIP! EXCEPT FOR ALL GREAT WORKS BY COMRADE DEREK PELL!**

One day your friend, Yo Bing, walks up to you wearing a Red Guard armband and carrying *The Little Red Book of Adobe LiveMotion.*

"Yo Bing! How you doin'?" (You've been reading too much Elmore Leonard.)

The unauthorized edition.

"Greetings, Comrade Wong. You will join us on our Long March to Ho Bok-in to serve the People in the fight against imperialist clowns and bandits!"

"Hoboken??? I'd rather sleep with the fishes."

"No, *idiot!*—Lodi Province, China."

"But that's 500 miles from here!"

"We must carry the Red Flag wherever Chairman Mao Teachings lie untaught."

"Come again?"

"Educate the masses in the 'Correct Way of Working with Objects in LiveMotion.' Before the People can *animate*, they must be taught to *subjugate* objects in the composition!"

"But the song says . . . 'it ain't the meat, it's the *motion*'?"

"Wong! *Objects* come first, then Flash!"

"Oh, *now* I get it. Let's go kick some object butt! . . ."

An Object is an Object is an Object . . .

What is a LiveMotion object?

Actually, the question should be: What *isn't* a LiveMotion object?

That is to say, an object in LiveMotion is just about everything.

Anything you create, draw, animate, drag, drop, import, or smuggle into the composition is an object. Be it vector or bitmap graphic, text, shape, path, or sound—*all* are objects, animated or not. Of course, without user intervention, they are just dumb objects—as dumb as that infamous remark made by President Nixon during his visit to China: "Mr. Zedong, tear down this Great Wall!"[3] They get smart as soon as you start manipulating them—select them, turn them into subversive groups, or combine and unite them to create new shapes.

Aligning Anarchist Objects in the Mass Struggle

"An undisciplined army marches backward into battle and gets its butt kicked. A disciplined army, aligned in spirit, marches forward to victory and looks good, too."

—Mao Zedong How to Win Wars and Influence Peoples [sic][4]

When it comes to disciplining an army of disorderly objects, LiveMotion can snap them into line and make them stand at attention and salute the Red flag.

With two or more objects selected in the composition, go to the menu under Object • Align and you'll find seven choices: Left, Right, Top, Bottom, Horizontal Centers, Vertical Centers, Centers. A glance at the chart in Figure 3-11 illustrates the results of each command when applied to three anarchist objects in their original position in the top left panel. (For the sake of clarity, the object's bounding boxes are not shown.)

Because the objects in the chart are irregularly shaped, the alignment does not appear precise in each instance as the command is based on the total dimensions of the object. But try this: Draw a rectangle (fill it with any color) and press CTRL-D twice to make two duplicates. Drag the top two rectangles away and position them anywhere in the composition. Then choose Horizontal Centers from the Align menu.

Since the objects are the same dimensions, one will be visible.

---

[3] This line will go down in history. Way down. Fortunately, Chairman Mao wasn't present to hear it, as he was too busy analyzing reports from his spies in the Nixon White House. Today, at least, Americans can take comfort in the fact that the current occupant of the White House, George W. Bush, is a man of carefully chosen words. Stupid words, but carefully chosen.
[4] Published by the People's Animation Army Press (1961) and distributed free to "volunteers."

Figure 3-11: Anarchist objects aligned.

Move each object to different positions and try the various alignments.

When designing Web navigation buttons, this feature is killer.

Crash Course in Subversively Grouping Objects

Why group objects?

Correct, Comrades—to save yourself time and effort!

Instead of selecting, say, a dozen objects individually to change their position, you can move them all en masse by grouping them. In addition to advancing an entire Red army division across the composition, with a single shot (mouse click) you can transform a rainbow coalition of vector objects into a unified color, animate them all, or apply a single Maoist style or texture. One caveat, you can't apply a style or texture to bitmap images, only to vectors.

What if some objects are standing in the way of those you wish to group?

Execute them. (Just kidding.)

Drag a marquee around the contiguous ones and SHIFT-CLICK on the others you wish to include. Then press CTRL-G to make the group. Now don't be fooled when a bounding box appears around all the objects—only the ones you selected are actually part of the group. Just click on any of the grouped objects (not the one[s] you've excluded) and drag. Your grouped objects will move while the outcast(s) remain stationary.

Again, to move a group, click on any of its *objects* and drag, *not* in the empty space within the bounding box which deselects the group.

When a group has outlived its usefulness in the great struggle, ungroup or disband it by selecting any one of its members and pressing CTRL-U (the "U" is for *Underground group.* Good move, Adobe!).

Now, let's say you have a gang of four Red Stars that you've organized as a Maoist group—then decide you want one to be black. What do you do?

You could press CTRL-U to ungroup them, select the object, change its color, drag a marquee around the whole gang again to regroup them, and press CTRL-G.

But why bother with all those steps when you've got the Subgroup Selection Tool?

Armed with the Subgroup Selection Tool, simply click the object you wish to isolate. It will then appear within its own bounding box, while the box around the group remains highlighted, but with a thick blue line (see Figure 3-12). After altering the object's

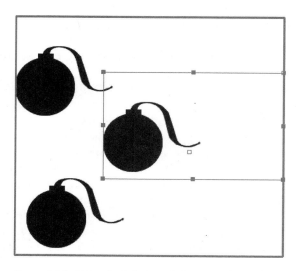

Figure 3-12: Using the Subgroup Selection tool to isolate an object.

color, switch back to the Selection tool and click an empty area in the composition (outside the bounding box).

Your objects are once again happily united, albeit no longer of uniform color.

Combining Objects for a United Front

By combining two or more *overlapping* objects, you can create an entirely new object. Whether it be type, shape, or bitmap image—all can be combined to produce cool Maoist morphs and contours.

From the Object • Combine menu (Figure 3-13), you have four[4] options: Unite, Unite with Color, Minus Front, Exclude. (Each option has its own icon, and if you find them helpful I'll eat my Mao cap.)

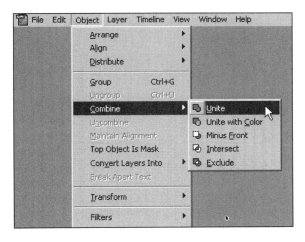

Figure 3-13: The Combine menu.

The Unite option combines the edges of selected objects.

The chart in Figure 3-14 shows a black blob overlapping a styled apple shape. Combing the two produces the deformed apple in the middle, since the bottom object always assumes the attributes of the top one. Reversing the objects results in the black mushy shape.

Unite with Color (Figure 3-15, upper left) doesn't change the shapes of the selected objects, but simply joins them.

Minus Font (Figure 3-15, upper right) deletes the outline of the top object from the one below.

---

[4] Rumor has it, the next version will include a fifth option: Ass Backward.

Intersect (Figure 3-15, lower left) removes all portions of the top object that are not overlapping.

Exclude (Figure 3-15, lower right) makes the overlapping portions of the top object transparent.

Figure 3-14: Combine and conquer.

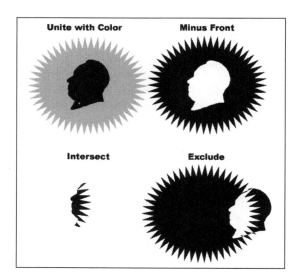

Figure 3-15: Assorted Combine options.

Aligning, Uniting, Combining for Victory

The chart in Figure 3-16, includes four Red Guard cheerleaders who haven't gotten their act together (top row).

By simply commanding them to *"Align Top!"* they are ready to march in lockstep and serve the Chairman, do or die (middle row).

By uniting them (lower left) or combining them (lower right), they have been made to rise above their peasant object roots into shapely, enlightened objects!

Figure 3-16: Aligning, uniting, and combining.

The final chart (Figure 3-17) shows you how to make a fast buck.

You need never feel shackled when working with objects in LiveMotion. The program's multiple undos, plus its Ungroup and Uncombine commands, should encourage you to experiment freely. So go forth and gather your objects in the composition. Spend a little time working with them and you'll quickly discover it's as much fun as playing with dolls (Figures 3-18 and 3-19).

Figure 3-17: Combining objects for fun and profit.

Figure 3-18: P.L.A. Joe Classic Collection.

Figure 3-19: Mao Action Figure Set.[5]

---

[5] Fully poseable and articulated, with detachable head. WARNING: CHOKING HAZARD.

*Chairman Mao presides over the grand opening of the
People's Liberation Library outside the Great Wall Mart.*

4

REVOLUTIONARY STYLES, TEXTURES, AND THE PEOPLE'S LIBERATION LIBRARY

As we saw in the previous chapter, the Adobe Motion Patrol (AMP) wisely, and with great cunning, fortified its Big Class-Smashing Weapon with a united front of People's palettes and vector tools. However, the cadres of Adobe programmers were not content to rest on their laurels and hearty tools but instead pushed forward bravely in the battle for Total Victory Over Deviant Stooges.

"All Cheap Rightist-Leftist Upside-Downists will be Beaten and Defeated!" they shouted, though the slogan made no sense.

What they undoubtedly intended to express was their commitment to empowering the People with supremely flexible library palettes, loaded with firepower in the form of preset shapes, icons, cult symbols, textures, and animations.

Three Cheers for the Gang of Four Palettes

Three cheers for the Gang of Four Palettes: Library, Textures, Styles, and Sounds. (We'll explore the first three here and save Sounds for Chapter 10, "The Great Wall of Sound.") All bundled under one pagoda (Figure 4-1), they appear like a shining edifice of Shanghai Tech—a fraternal factory where lackluster objects are

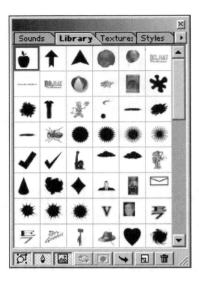

Figure 4-1: The Gang of Four Palettes.

reborn as Red Flag–waving warriors. Each palette is stocked with specimens that far surpass mere filler. Indeed, the Motion Patrol was clearly guided by a desire to ignite the end user's imagination.

The People's Liberation Library

Think of the Library palette as a shrine for model workers—a shelter for all those innovative objects (and groups of objects) you wish to use over and over—for example, Web site navigation bars, Mao buttons, subversive shapes, icons, cult figures, and logos. All can be safely stored in the People's Liberation Library. (No library card, no overdue fines, no firing squads!)

Generously, Adobe stocked the Library with an assortment of useful shapes to get you started: arrows, blobs, figures, stars, and so on. These vector objects can be scaled up or down, rotated, stretched, colored, distorted, embossed, endlessly transformed, and animated.

To add your own creations to the Library, all you need do is draw a shape or import an image into your composition. Select and drag it directly into the Library palette. A box will pop up, enabling you to type a unique name for your object.

You can drag and drop objects from your desktop or another application, or click the New Object button at the bottom of the palette to choose an item from any location on your computer.

White Bone Demon

LiveMotion has a habit of making imported/placed/dragged content match whatever is selected in the composition when it's brought in. If you paste when a shape is selected or drag an object onto that shape, LiveMotion will cause the shape's object layer to be filled with the new image. It will also adjust the incoming image's dimensions based on whatever is selected. If you wish to avoid this behavior, remember to deselect before you import.

Figure 4-2 shows a copy of my design for a new cereal box in honor of Los Alamos (Cheaties: Breakfast of Chinese Spies) being dragged directly from Photoshop (left) into LiveMotion (right) in preparation for enshrinement in the People's Library.

Figure 4-2: The Adobe One-Step Drag & Drop from Photoshop to LiveMotion.

When you need to raid the Library, just scroll through the collection until you find the appropriate swatch (thumbnail). Select and drag it to the composition (see Figure 4-3).

If dragging and dropping strikes you as counterrevolutionary, use the more civilized Place Object button at the bottom of the palette. It's as quick and easy as Instant Red Guard Rice.

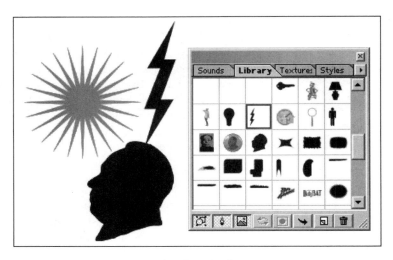

Figure 4-3: Assorted objects dragged into battle.

As your collection blossoms into a shining Red Army of activist objects, finding what you're looking for may become like searching for a chopstick in a haystack. In the default Swatches view, you may find it difficult to differentiate between objects of similar shape and color. You can change views by clicking the small arrow in the upper right corner of the palette. Select either Preview, to see a list of the objects by name and a single thumbnail of whatever object you highlight, or Name view, which presents multiple thumbnails and the name of each object. For easy identification, use unique, descriptive names when adding objects to the Library. For example, instead of simply labeling an object "Heart," name it "Throbbing Beveled Heart Bursting with Revolutionary Pride". . . .

When the Library becomes overcrowded, you can use the three buttons located at the lower left of the palette: View LiveMotion Objects, View Vector Objects, and View Image Objects. Limiting the palette's view to one of these three categories will facilitate the quick location of items. Of course, if you end up storing hundreds of different Mao badges, locating the right one will be problematic. With a little luck, the forces at Adobe are hard at work fortifying the People's Library with its own mini-search engine. But just in case they're not, send an email to the LiveMotion Wish List—livemotionwishlist@adobe.com—and politely request a Library search function.

Or . . . threaten to launch a Rectification Campaign!

Additional Library Palette Buttons

Other palette buttons provide additional access to objects. For example, Replace Object (the twin arrows) will replace any selected object in the composition with whatever object you click on in the Library. You can also replace any object by dragging another object into its place. Be aware, however, that LiveMotion will fit the new artwork into the dimensions of the old.

The Make Active Matte button is a truly exciting weapon. It allows you to take any shape in the Library and apply it as a matte to another object—even objects created in outside applications, such as Photoshop and Illustrator. In Figure 4-4, I've imported a bitmap image of Mao's wife, Jiang Qing (pronounced *white-bone demon*) and applied a Blotch matte. Appropriately, it appears as if her image is being erased.[1]

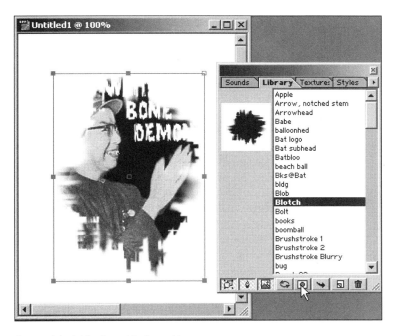

Figure 4-4: A blotch on Madame Mao.

Try importing your own images and applying various shapes as mattes. Experiment freely and you'll discover a myriad of possibilities for use in your layouts, designs, and animations.

---

[1] Revisionism in action!

In addition to keeping static vectors and bitmaps handy, the Library can even store animated objects. That makes it a motion library in the truest sense. We'll put this radical resource to good use in Chapter 7.

Use the People's Library wisely, and you'll find it's worth more than all the tea in China.

March of the Billion Styles Brigade

As evidenced by the magnificent images throughout this book, Chairman Mao cut a dashing (albeit corpulent) figure. Despite a drab wardrobe and a penchant for the simplicity of his peasant roots, Mao Zedong had style and charisma to the max. (How else to explain the success of his Little Red Book?)[2] Yet what is style—that nebulous thing we all aspire to but few of us achieve? Happily, you don't need to beat your brains out consulting dusty tomes of Marxism–Leninism–Mao Zedong Thought for the answer—LiveMotion comes armed with a variety of preset styles that you can easily apply to any object or gang of objects.

Briefly, styles are collections of attributes, properties, and effects that transform a drab object (shape, text, or image) into a Communist Party animal. These attributes (colors, shadows, backgrounds, fills, textures, and animations) appear on separate layers (viewable in the Object palette) that can be turned off and on as you please. They are nondestructive—that is, the object always retains its original, editable characteristics. A style *does not* change the shape of an object but adds character and zest via the various attributes.

The Styles palette (Figure 4-5) also comes loaded with preset animations, so without even touching LiveMotion's utopian Timeline, you can instantly animate an object and impress your fellow workers.

Let's animate a little red apple in honor of the Great Helmsman.

1. Start a new composition, using the default settings.

2. From the Window menu, choose Reset to Defaults to align the palettes and return all settings to their original configuration.

3. In the Color palette, move the top slider bar all the way to the right, setting the object fill color to bright red.

---

[2] From 1966 to 1968, over 740,000,000 copies of the Chinese edition were printed. By the year 2084, *The Little Red Book of Adobe LiveMotion* will have easily surpassed that figure.

Figure 4-5: The Styles palette.

4. In the Library palette, highlight the thumbnail depicting an apple. At the bottom of the palette, click the Place Object button to propel a copy of the object to the center of the composition. Like a Red Guard Guided Missile, the apple instantly strikes its target.

5. Select the Styles tab and click the small arrow in the palette's upper right corner. From the drop-down list, choose Name view so the styles are presented in clear, alphabetical order. Double-click "anim arc fade left". A series of blue dots and squares appears alongside the apple, depicting the path and keyframes of the preset animation.

6. Believe it or not, you've already animated the apple. To test the animation, click the Preview Mode button at the bottom of the Toolbox.

7. Give yourself a pat on the back—you've created your first motion graphic!

8. To exit Preview mode, click the Edit Mode button on the Toolbox next to the Preview Mode button.

But wait—*the apple has vanished!* Only its bounding box and animation path are visible.

Relax. It's not a plot by the Gang of Four; it's actually a convenient feature. Whenever you switch from Preview to Edit mode, the program automatically returns to the animation's first frame. In our example, the apple is invisible because we chose a preset that fades *in* the object as it arcs right and bounces.

Quick Timeline Preview

Although we'll explore the Timeline in detail in the next chapter, let's jump the gun and take a sneak peek now. Military drum roll, please. . . .

Press CTRL-T to display the Timeline (Figure 4-6).

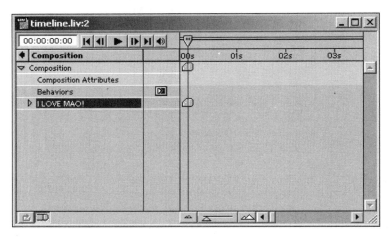

Figure 4-6: The Timeline unveiled.

NOTE *If the Timeline window obscures your view of the composition, minimize, move, or resize it as you would any other standard window.*

I can hear oohing and ahhhing, as if I'd unveiled a nuclear warhead at the May Day parade. Well, I have.

Take a moment to admire its modernized design. Sing loud the praises of the Shining Red Guard Timeline Troop (a.k.a. the Adobe LiveMotion Development Team).

If this is your first animation program, the Timeline may seem foreign to you, but bear in mind that, unlike the timeline in Macromedia Flash, this one is intuitive and efficient, and you'll master it quickly. Also, take comfort in the fact that I come to LiveMotion as a rebellious artist, not as technocrat nor as geek. If this were rocket science, my book would not exist.

Notice the words *Red Geometric* on the left of the Timeline's composition column. That's Adobe-speak for *red apple*, which—although invisible at the moment—is the object currently selected in the composition. In the upper left corner is the Current Time window (00:00:00:00), and directly to its right are the playback controls. These four arrows will be familiar to everyone who has used a Walkman or VCR.

Click the last arrow on the right (next to the speaker icon) and take a Great Leap Forward to the animation's final frame. Presto—our little red apple reappears!

You could have achieved the same effect by clicking the current time marker (CTM), the thin red line in the Timeline window, and dragging it to the right.

Try moving the CTM back and forth manually to step backward and forward one frame at a time. This operation is commonly referred to as "scrubbing" by professional animators and is a handy way to deconstruct a movie's motion flow.

If the above doesn't whet your appetite to launch a motion graphics attack, consider this: If LiveMotion were a country—say, China—the Timeline would be Beijing. It's the very heart and soul of the program and the key to producing immortal motion graphics. Therefore, skip Chapter 5, "Timeline Ballet," at your own Red Peril.

More on Styles

For now, let's return to styles. Close both the Timeline and composition windows and start fresh.

1. Open a blank composition with the default settings.

2. Select any color from the Color palette.

3. Using the Polygon tool, click in the composition and drag to create a shape.

4. In the Properties palette, move the Sides slider bar to the left and set it to 3. You now have a triangle.

5. In the Styles palette, select Preview mode by clicking the little arrow in the upper right, and then locate and highlight Four-way Blend.

6. Click the Apply Style button.

   Pretty snazzy, no?

Viewing Style Layers

Glance at the Object palette and you'll see that the Four-way Blend preset style comprises five separate layers—four textures and a soft drop shadow. By clicking the eyeball icons in the Object palette, you can view the individual effects each layer has on the texture. Thanks to LiveMotion, you've been spared the time and effort normally required to create these effects.

Customizing a Style

Now let's customize this preset Style and make it our own.

1. In the Object palette, highlight the first layer (Texture 1) and turn it off by clicking the eyeball icon. Do the same with Texture 3. This hides the golden gradient and reveals a blue, tiled bulb pattern.

2. In the 3D palette, choose Bevel from the menu. Using the sliders, set the bevel's Depth to 17, the Softness to 0, and the Lighting to 132.

3. Use the slider bar controls in the Adjust palette to set the Brightness level to 121, the Contrast to –24, the Saturation to –80, and the Tint to 160.

4. With the triangle still selected in the composition, click the New Style button in the Styles palette and enter a name for the customized style (such as Beveled Blue Tile). Make sure the Ignore Color of First Layer option is unchecked, and then click OK. Bingo! You've created a unique style that you can now apply to any object. If you want to save the triangular shape itself for use as a button, simply drag it into the Library palette. (See Figure 4-7.)

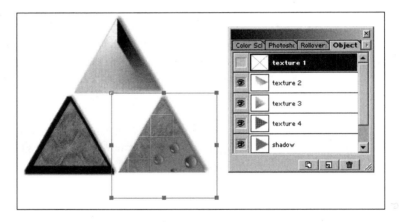

Figure 4-7: Eternal triangles with layer effects.

Now we're going to get rid of this shape but place its appearance on a new shape.

1. Click DELETE to remove the object from the composition window.

2. Select the Ellipse tool and, holding down the SHIFT key, draw a circle. (If you don't hold down SHIFT you'll draw an ellipse.)

3. In the Styles palette, locate your new style, highlight it, and click the Apply Style button. You've now got a round button with your customized style applied.

Copying and Pasting Styles

Now let's create some revolutionary slogans with one of Live-Motion's coolest features: the ability to copy and paste styles.

1. With the round button from the previous exercise selected, press CTRL-C (Copy).

2. Press T for the Type tool, and click on a blank area of the composition to bring up the Text dialog box. Change the font from its default to something bold and brazen like Arial Black. Set the size to 30. In the text area, type the following slogan: LONG LIVE CHAIRMAN MAO! (See Figure 4-8.)

Figure 4-8: Propaganda slogan, before and after cosmetic surgery.

3. Click OK to close the dialog box and send the text to the composition. If necessary, tap the V key to get the Selection arrow, and then select and reposition the text so it's completely visible.

4. With the text selected, right-click anywhere on the slogan and choose Paste Style from the menu.

The unique ability to copy and paste styles between objects is one of LiveMotion's most incredible features. You can also copy and paste textures as well as animations. The Chairman himself would be tickled pink.

Textures: Footprints on the Road to Liberation

Once, while gazing at a pre-Liberation photograph of Shenyang, Chairman Mao was heard to remark, "The road from feudal village to revolutionary citadel is but a billion footprints in the dust, give or take a few million."

Although its meaning is unclear, the quotation remains memorable simply because the Chairman said it.

Just as these proverbial footprints conjure up images of revolutionary fervor, textures add life to vector shapes and text. Like its styles, Adobe's preset textures can be modified and saved, or you can create your own and store them in the Textures palette. This palette functions in the same manner as its neighbors, but it has two unique buttons, which I'll explain in a bit.

NOTE *If you intend to export to Flash, remember that textures and effects will export as bitmaps, resulting in larger files.*

Let's liberate a plain vanilla background with one of Adobe's radical presets.

1. Start a new composition and size it 500 x 500.

2. Maximize the new composition window so that it's surrounded by a gray workspace.

3. Using the Rectangle tool, drag a rectangle so that it covers the entire composition.

4. In the Textures palette, choose Name view and scroll through the swatches until you come to Twirlypeat. This is one of my favorites, and you'll find it in use on this book's companion site (www.littleredbooks.com).

5. Click inside the swatch and drag your cursor to the composition. (Or use the Apply Texture button.) Release the mouse button and you'll have a weird twirly-tiled background.

You'll find two buttons on the bottom left of the Textures palette: View Small Textures and View Big Textures. These divide the preset textures into those that are less than 500 x 500 pixels, and must be tiled to fill the background, and behemoths that will cover the composition without tiling.

White Bone Demon

Be cautious when using textured backgrounds in layouts. They can overpower text and images or clash with other design elements like fractious Red Guard units vying for the Chairman's attention. You can often avoid such turmoil by setting images and text in a smaller rectangle filled with a solid color that contrasts well with the textured background.

To produce the tiled Mao background shown in Figure 4-9, I dragged a small image of the Chairman from my desktop, dumped it unceremoniously into the Textures palette, and named it "mao". After creating a rectangle, I dragged Mao from the palette into the rectangle.

Nothing to it—multiple Maos!

Go forth now and practice, Comrades. You are well equipped with new weapons—vector drawing tools and power palettes.

Prepare to advance into Full Motion Revolt!

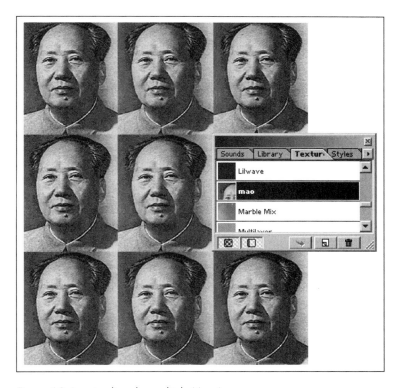

Figure 4-9: Leaping lizards—multiple Maos!

"Thoroughly smash the old way! Animate and liberate!"

5

TIMELINE BALLET: Orchestrating the Motion Revolution

It's as clear as the wart on the Chairman's chin—LiveMotion is a sleek and supple design environment. Yet beneath its placid interface lies a wonder weapon, capable of conquering all impudent SWF-snakes and GIF-devils. It's a long-range, antiballistic, tween-screaming, motion-blowing, golden-gleaming, animation master: the LiveMotion Timeline.

Fandong Bailei Jianjue Yao Gongpo.[1]

If the forces of Macromedia have anything to fear, it's the LiveMotion Timeline—the motion control center for all your animations.

During the arduous Long March through Silicon Valley, the Great Teacher Chairman Mao often paused for liquid refreshment and animation indoctrination. Once, while attempting to *tween* (insert frames between keyframes) in Macromedia Flash, he grew frustrated. His face turned red as he threw down his mouse, spilled his Red Jolt Cola, and roared, *"This Timeline is no dinner party!"*

---

[1] The reactionary fortress must be resolutely attacked and smashed.

Indeed, the Flash Timeline has forced many industrious students and workers to throw up their hands in defeat. Adrift in a sea of inscrutable commands, they longed for a simpler tool that would lead them to victory. Sure, Flash is a formidable weapon in the hands of code-snorting geeks addicted to ActionScript, but for the Masses (us common artists and Web graphics beginners) it's anti-intuitive and has a big, steep bourgeois learning curve.

By contrast, Adobe's Timeline is People-Friendly, adhering to strict Mao Zedong design principles. With hearts red like fire, youthful Red Guard cadres eagerly advance to their keyboards and launch the LiveMotion Timeline with glee.

Why such zealous dedication to a single feature? Because it automates manual labor and operates according to (believe it or not) Common Sense! Rather than forcing you to insert each keyframe[2] by hand to animate an object, LiveMotion's auto-tweening feature interpolates all the necessary frames to produce fluid movement. The user is free to focus attention on what matters most—the animation itself—while avoiding a quagmire of bourgeois technicalities.

A Journey of a Thousand Miles Begins with a Single Keyframe

Think of an animation as a disparate band of bitmaps and vectors, marching 6,000 miles from Jiangxi to Shaanxi Province. In this motion drama, each object (along with its many attributes) must take a first step (that is, the first keyframe) before reaching its destination. Some, like the redness in the disappearing apple in Chapter 4, will grow weary and exit before the final frame. Others will join in at various points along the path to victory. Some will spin, jump, bounce, or skew. Some will zoom in, others will shrink and disappear. Some will march apart like loners, some will move in groups. Some will carry protest banners, while others will chant or sing "Chairman Mao songs." And they all do this on the glorious Timeline.

You are the master of the LiveMotion Timeline, the leader orchestrating your objects' and their attributes' march though time. You should know where you are going and what the animation will look like when you get there—but, thanks to keyframes and the Timeline, you don't have to worry about every pit stop along the way.

Say, for example, you decide to create a visual motion-poem in which a fat capitalist roader is transformed into a tiny, impotent frog-demon. You place your capitalist roader, be he vector or

---

[2] A keyframe is an animation frame that defines a key object property at its position on the Timeline.

bitmap, in the composition at the precise point on the Timeline you wish him to appear. Then you select the particular attributes to be transformed (for example, scale and skew) and move to the frame at the point on the Timeline where the transformation should be complete. That, in a nutshell, is the process.

One Chopstick, One Keyframe . . . *No Dice!*

There's an old Chinese proverb that goes something like: *"Give a fat man one chopstick, and he'll soon learn to starve."*

OK, I confess; I made that up. Nevertheless, it's helpful when pondering the nature of keyframes. Keyframes are like waypoints; they denote the points in time where things change, just like pins on a map show changes in a path.

One keyframe, *no movement.* It's that simple. It takes two to tango; it takes two to conspire. And it takes at least two keyframes to make an animation: one to define the starting characteristics, the other to define the final characteristics. Keyframes don't simply mark the beginning and end of an animation; they're interspersed throughout the Timeline and contain all of the data that defines how each object behaves (which object properties change, at what point in time changes occur, the specific values of the changes, and the nature of the object's movement).

In between the start and stop keyframes are the common foot soldiers we can all take for granted, thanks to LiveMotion. As you transform an object's shape, size, and opacity and send it flying across the screen, LiveMotion automatically inserts the frames of the animation that come between the keyframes for you.

Although initially generated automatically whenever you transform an object attribute, keyframes can also be controlled manually, as you'll see in the cloud exercise later in this chapter.

One Timeline, Four Zones

Let's take a close look at the Timeline. Figure 5-1 shows the Timeline divided into four bite-sized sections:

1. **Motion control zone.** Directly below the current filename at the upper left of the Timeline is the Current Time window, which displays the animation time in hours, minutes, seconds, and frames. To the right of the Current Time window are the five playback controls: Start (which rewinds to the first frame), Previous Frame, Play, Next Frame, and End. Next to the playback controls is the Volume button, which turns the soundtrack on or off during playback.

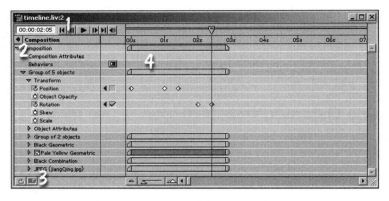

Figure 5-1: Crypto-Marxist deconstruction of the Timeline.

2. **Timeline Navigator and the object hierarchy.** The Navigator (the solid arrow pointing left) displays the name of the currently active Timeline and can toggle between the main composition and independent animation groups. (For information on *Time-Independent Groups,* see Chapter 8.) Below the Navigator is the object hierarchy, where each object in the animation is listed along with its attributes. (You must first click a twisty to see the associated attributes.)

3. **Great Loop Forward and the zoom zone.** Clicking the Loop button (located in the lower left corner) causes the animation to cycle continuously. Clicking the Auto-Length button, to the immediate right of the Loop button, extends the selected object's duration to the final frame of the animation and changes the Timeline length from Implicit to Explicit.[3] The three buttons with triangles on them are zoom controls that let you zoom in, out, and to the end of the Timeline.

4. **Timeline zone.** This is the belly of the beast, containing the composition's duration bar (depicting the length of the entire animation) and individual duration bars for each object. Represented by diamond-shaped icons on the duration bars, keyframes hold the data-defining object properties at that

---

[3] Undocumented Secret. Implicit vs. explicit length is not covered in the Live-Motion User Guide. Here's the scoop: most new items on the Timeline are set to implicit length; that is, they just appear at a certain point and continue to exist until the whole movie ends. Their length has never been specified explicitly, so they grow and shrink as the composition grows and shrinks. But if you click the Auto-Length button to set it to explicit, you can set their end points explicitly (you'll notice that the end cap of the item's duration bar becomes more sharply beveled and is consistent with the explicitly set duration of the composition).

position on the Timeline. The long, thin vertical line is the Current Time Marker (CTM), positioned at 02:03 on the Timeline in Figure 5-1.

Use the Timeline to Create an Animation

Let's create a simple storm cloud animation using the Timeline.

Lay the Groundwork

1. Start a new composition and size it at 650 x 400 pixels.
2. Press CTRL-S and name the file "cloud.liv." (Keep this file handy, as we'll use it again in Chapter 10.)
3. With the Color palette in RGB view, enter the following color values: 144 R, 151 G, and 150 B.
4. From the Toolbox, select the Paint Bucket tool and click anywhere inside the composition window to fill the background with this appropriately moody shade of gray.
5. Now we need an ominous cloud. Of course, we could draw one using the vector tools, but let's take the easy path (don't worry; Mao will never know) and use LiveMotion's preset clouds.

Add a Preset Cloud

You'll find two preset clouds waiting for you in the Library palette. Before choosing one, set your fill color to black by clicking inside the small black rectangle in the lower right corner of the Color palette (in RGB view).

1. Highlight either Cloud1 or Cloud2 in the Library list.
2. Insert the cloud by clicking the palette's Place Object button.
3. Using the Selection tool, reposition the cloud in the upper left corner of the composition.
4. With the cloud selected, launch the Timeline by pressing CTRL-T. (You may have to resize both the Timeline and the composition windows for easier access.)[4]

Animate the Cloud

The Timeline now has two duration bars—one (light gray) for the entire composition and the other pink for our cloud object. Every object in an animation will have its own duration bar, apart from

---

[4] Consider investing in a large monitor (19 to 21 inches) to give yourself ample room to animate.

the ever-present composition bar. Each duration bar contains a pair of start and end markers that can be dragged horizontally to extend the duration bar.

1. Notice that our cloud is highlighted in the object hierarchy list. By default, the label Black Geometric has been applied to the cloud. Let's change the name by pressing ENTER. Type "Black Cloud" in the pop-up dialog box. Press ENTER again to close the window.

2. Click the little "twisty" (triangle) to the left of Black Cloud; this is the Expand/Collapse control. It expands to show a list of the object's properties: Transform, Object Attributes, and Layer. Clicking the triangle a second time closes the list.[5]

3. Click the twisty next to Transform to reveal the Gang of Five— Position, Object Opacity, Rotation, Skew, and Scale (see Figure 5-2). These are the most common object attributes and often the most efficient to animate because they're native in the Flash (.swf) format. You'll quickly learn to appreciate them as reliable comrades.

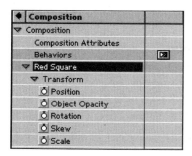

Figure 5-2: The Gang of Five Transform attributes.

NOTE   *Clicking the little stopwatch icon beside each attribute inserts an initial keyframe (represented by a diamond) on the Timeline at whatever point you've positioned the CTM. By clicking the Stopwatch you're essentially telling LiveMotion to "listen" to the changes you make to that attribute at that given point in time. If you later decide to delete a particular attribute's transformation, simply click*

---

[5] When you're animating numerous objects, the contents of the Timeline will extend well beyond the bottom border of your screen. As you move from object to object, you'll need to "collapse" the twisties to hide the lists of properties and to avoid constant scrolling. You can also nest objects in groups for more efficient Timeline management. See Chapter 8 for more on nested objects.

the checked box next to the attribute and its keyframes will be removed. You can also highlight individual keyframes and forcibly reeducate them by pressing the DELETE *key.*

4. Our sample animation will run for six seconds. In the Timeline, drag the end marker of the duration bar to 06s on the Timeline. To make it longer, just drag the CTM further down the Timeline.

> **NOTE** *Even though LiveMotion lets you specify timing with some precision, timing is kind of a fuzzy concept both inside the authoring tool and in the Flash player. Both environments will endeavor to play the animation at the desired frame rate but may fall behind in complex animations. Luckily, if you find that you've chosen a too-demanding frame rate, you can reduce it without changing the timing settings of your animation. For example, whereas Flash would make a 1-second animation 3 seconds if you changed the frame rate from 30 to 10 fps, LiveMotion would keep it at 1 second and just reduce the number of frames. In general, however, player speed issues are most important when trying to synch sound. See Chapter 10 for more on this subject.*

Make the Cloud Appear from Afar

Now let's make the animation begin with the cloud set off in the distance.

1. In the Timeline, drag the CTM to the beginning of the animation (all the way to the left).

2. Make sure the cloud is selected in the composition window. In the Transform palette, change the cloud's dimensions to 49 x 21.

3. In the hierarchy list, click the stopwatch next to the Scale attribute to insert a start keyframe for the cloud's size (scale).

4. Drag the CTM to 03s (the 3-second mark), halfway through our animation.

5. Place your cursor in the composition window above the lower right handle of the cloud's bounding box. Holding the Shift key, click and drag downward to resize the cloud to its original size (280 x 122). A glance at the Transform palette will show you the object's dimensions as you resize it.

6. Use the Start and Play controls to view the animation.

   Our cloud comes to life!

If you want to accelerate the cloud's movement, select the Position keyframe at 03s in the Timeline and drag it closer to the start keyframe. Try moving the keyframe to various positions and then playing the animation to see how each affects the object's movement.

Stormy Weather

Let's kick the animation up another notch.

1. Click the Start button to return to the first frame.
2. In the hierarchy list, click the Position stopwatch.
3. Drag the CTM back to 03s.
4. With the Selection tool, select the cloud and, keeping it at the top of the composition, move it horizontally to the center.
5. Preview the animation.

Now for a Dash of Drama . . .

Let's add a lightning bolt to our scene and make it flash by animating the bolt's opacity.

Add the Lightning Bolt

1. Move the CTM to 04s.
2. In the Library palette, locate the vector lightning bolt and place it in the composition. With the object selected, press ENTER and name it "Lightning." Press ENTER again to close the dialog box.
3. Choose a dark shade of red from the Color palette to change the bolt from black to red.
4. Reposition the bolt so it extends from the center of the cloud and slightly overlaps the cloud's edge.
5. From the Object menu, choose Arrange • Send to Back. This moves the bolt behind the cloud. Your scene should now look like Figure 5-3.

Animate the Bolt's Opacity

In the hierarchy list, click the triangle next to Lightning to reveal a list of Lightning's attributes. With the bolt selected, click Object Opacity.

In the Opacity palette, drag the Object Opacity bar to the left to set it at 0. The bolt is now invisible, but its bounding box remains so we know it's still there.

Figure 5-3: The cloud scene with lightning bolt.

In the Timeline, move the CTM just to the right of the new keyframe (00:00:04:01). Return to the Opacity palette and set the Object Opacity back to 100.

Duplicate the Opacity Keyframes

To make the lightning bolt flash effectively, we must duplicate the Opacity keyframes we've just added. We could repeat the previous steps, but that would be slow and counterrevolutionary. Live-Motion can copy the keyframes for us!

1. Place your cursor just above and to the left of the two keyframes; click and drag to select them. Holding down the ALT key, click either of the highlighted diamonds and drag them to the right. This produces a duplicate set. (Don't worry if the diamonds overlap slightly.)

2. Repeat above step for all the keyframes.

3. Finally, select the first keyframe and, holding ALT, drag a copy to the end of the Timeline. You now have a total of nine keyframes, the first and last reflecting the object at zero opacity.

4. Using the playback controls, rewind and preview the animation.

5. Save it!

Congratulations! You've successfully animated a Glorious Red Flash of Lighting. But surely our test animation could be made to more effectively serve the People. How, you ask? By adding a dramatic clap of thunder.

So if you're feeling heroic, skip to Chapter 10 to learn how to work with audio files.

"Politically Correct" Moves: Auto Bezier and Linear Motion

Controlling an object's motion path can be as critical as controlling the trajectory of a PRC missile. Most often, you'll want your objects to travel smoothly through the composition, like the cloud you just animated. Because of this, Adobe has made its default motion Auto Bezier. (Vector art is made up of Bezier curves.) However, when you want your object to move at sharp angles and in straight lines, right-click the object's keyframe and choose Linear from the shortcut menu.

Once an object has been animated, you can select it to see its animation path and keyframes (represented by blue dots) in the composition window. You'll notice that if you raise the frame rate of your animation, LiveMotion inserts more frames and you therefore see more dots.

Figure 5-4 shows a PAA[6] rocket with a Linear motion path. In Figure 5-5, the rocket is shown in Auto Bezier mode—a smooth, albeit suicidal, path.

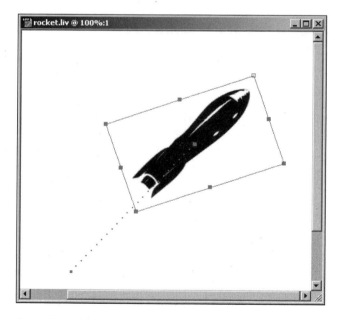

Figure 5-4: PAA rocket with Linear motion path.

---

[6] People's Animation Army.

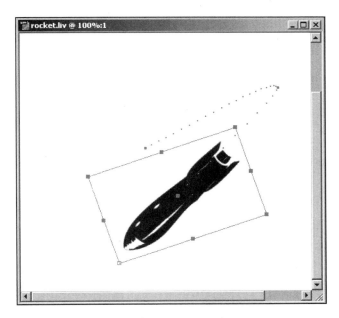

Figure 5-5: PAA rocket with Auto Bezier path.

Nerd Perfect

Let me digress a bit here and take you back in timeline.

I began my life as an artist working with paper, scissors, and spray adhesive. Being self-uneducated, my medium of choice was collage. I was inspired by the Gang of Four—not *the* Gang of Four but rather my own personal gang: Alfred Jarry, Alphonse Allais, Marcel Duchamp, and Max Ernst. The first two were great absurdist writers and the latter two, experimental visual artists.

After years of painful paper cuts and brain damage caused by inhaling adhesive, I discovered computers—the perfect medium for collage!

Using Photoshop, I was able to produce literally thousands of digital images that—had they been done by hand—would have consumed two lifetimes. My very first digital work was titled *Nerd Descending a Staircase* (Figure 5-6)—an intentionally bitmapped homage to Duchamp's Cubist classic.[7]

Flash forward to the present (Figure 5-7). LiveMotion has enabled me to revise my work and bring it to life as a 9K Flash animation.

---

[7] *Nude Descending a Staircase* (1912); a smashing motion graphic without the motion!

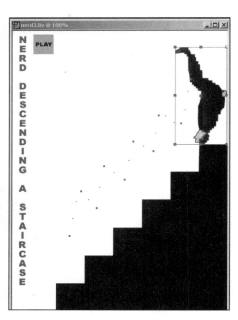

Figure 5-6: Nerd Descending a Staircase.   *Figure 5-7: Original LiveMotion file.*

To view the animation (and hopefully have a few chuckles), go to the Little Red Books Web site at www.littleredbooks.com/nerd.htm.

Since *Nerd* employs several animation techniques covered later on, we'll use it again, so be sure to download the original LiveMotion file (nerd.liv). You'll find a link to the download at the URL just given.

I scanned the nerd directly into Photoshop from my original grayscale graphic. There I created a path of the figure, and I then placed the layered file into LiveMotion. The staircase was drawn with LiveMotion's Pen tool, as was the button. Finally, I added the text.

For the benefit of those who didn't rush right off to the Little Red Books Web site to view the animation, the nerd is activated by a green rollover play button in the upper left corner. As you may have guessed, he descends the staircase one step at a time, on his head. When he reaches the bottom, there's an oh-so-brief pause before he snaps instantly back to the top of the stairs and waits for the viewer's input.

As you can see, this is an example of interactivity at its most basic. Delete the button from the scene, and we'd have a plain vanilla motion graphic. Had I opted to have the animation loop, it would have immediately grown tiresome.

Figure 5-8 shows how I transformed only the nerd's Position attribute with eleven keyframes. Note the circled keyframe. The left-pointing arrow indicates that an Ease Out transition was applied to the keyframe. (I did this via a right-click.) This transition adds a slight delay before the nerd whisks back to the top of the stairs. Had I not added the Ease Out transition, the motion would have been too abrupt. Subtle tweaks in the Timeline often make the difference between a successful animation and a flop.

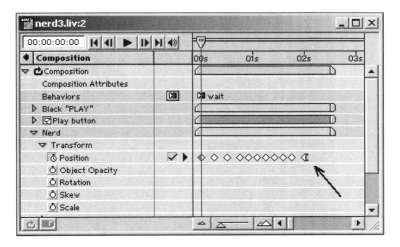

Figure 5-8: Nerd *keyframes.*

Throughout the rest of this book we'll pay frequent visits to Adobe's wonder weapon. After all, the Timeline is where the action is.

Cultural Revolution ad campaign poster.

6

TEXTUAL MISCHIEF AND THE ART OF PROPAGANDA:
Animating Words and Text

Ahhh . . . there is nothing like the fine art of Chinese written propaganda. Nothing, that is, except American advertising copy. You may never have used *Red Guard Deodorant*, but you undoubtedly remember the slogan (see Figure 6-1). Beijing's Ministry of Propaganda and Madison Avenue have always had a lot in common. In fact, you might say they're comrades-in-ads.

Deep down in his little red heart, Mao knew that everyone—even hardcore communards—live by selling something; whether it's baking soda, a book of quotations, or world revolution—*everything must go.* Hyperbolic phrases serve to cloud critical faculties with massive hex appeal. For example, if I announced that my Little Red Book *weighs a ton*, you'd assume you were getting more for your money.

When creating motion graphics, we sometimes overlook text in favor of animating pictures. Thus, text is relegated to mere caption status—static and perfunctory.

The People's Animation Army knows that *action text* can incite the masses to break free of their chains and rise up in revolt.

See Mao and his capitalist running dog, Spot.

See them run.

Run, Mao, run!

See, Spot runs faster than his master.[1]

Figure 6-1: "Imperialism Stinks!" campaign poster.

Image from Dick and Jane and Other Running Dog Imperialists.

Animating text can also kill two words with one stone, captivating an audience through visual presentation while delivering a message faster via smaller file sizes. Text animations let you use any font on your system and will embed the font in your LiveMotion file, so others can view it even if they don't have the font.

The Type Tool

LiveMotion's Type tool is as straightforward as a barefoot doctor. Simply click the T icon on the toolbar, click anywhere in the composition, and ye shall receive the Type Tool dialog box, shown in Figure 6-2.

---

[1] From *Dick and Jane and Other Running Dog Imperialists: A Little Red Guard Primer,* edited by Derek Pell (Beijing: 1969). Went out of print during the Propaganda Famine of 1972.

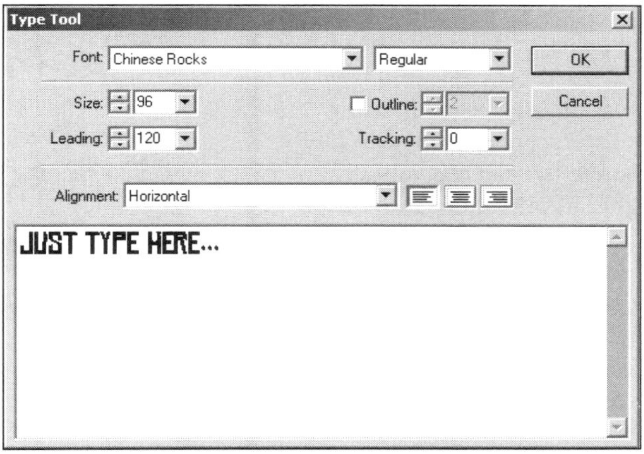

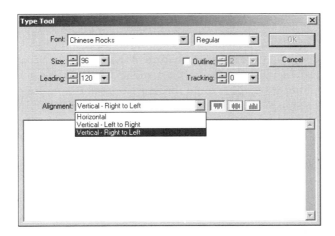

Figure 6-2: The Type Tool dialog box.

The choices in this dialog box are fairly standard type properties: font, style (regular, bold, italic), size, leading, and tracking.
(Leading is the amount of vertical space between the baselines in
lines of text; tracking is the amount of horizontal space between
each letter.) You can also choose the Outline option for type without a fill color. You don't set the type's color here, but rather in
the Color palette.

The Alignment feature (Figure 6-3) enables you to have text
appear vertically from left to right or vice versa. This is particularly
handy when you have to create a big Chinese character poster
extolling the virtues of Mao Zedong Thought, as in Figure 6-4.

Figure 6-3: Setting type alignment.

Text that you enter appears in the composition window at the position where you clicked. You can, of course, reposition it anywhere by selecting and dragging it, or you can move it in precise increments via the Transform palette's X and Y coordinates. This palette also lets you stretch, rotate, and skew text and adjust letter spacing with precision.

As with the Type Tool dialog box, you can make basic changes to your type (font, size, and so forth) in the Properties palette.

To quickly edit content, select the text in your composition and double-click to bring up the Type Tool dialog box.[2]

Figure 6-4: Big Chinese character poster.

Six Red Anagrams = Marx, as in Grades!

Let's look at a simple text animation to whet your appetite. For this example, I began by creating six anagrams. (An anagram is a word or phrase formed by rearranging the letters of another word or phrase.) My goal was to find rich, ironic phrases that would amuse and entertain you. (Easier said than done, believe me.) Taking my own advice from Chapter 2, I began with pencil and paper[3] before launching LiveMotion. At first, my focus was not on design but rather on the nature of the text I'd be bringing to life. If the text itself failed to spark the imagination, it would hardly matter if I made it zoom through hoops and perform cartwheels.

Once I had a finished "script," the question became how best to present it. I decided it would be effective to have the original words from which the anagrams were made fade in, one at a time, from the top of the list to the bottom. To add contrast to the simple black-and-white composition, I set the fade-in text color to red.

---

[2] By the time you read this, Adobe will probably have done away with the Type Tool dialog box altogether—just as it's done in Photoshop 6—and you'll simply click and type. If so, let's give them a cheer!
[3] Organize! Organize! Organize!

Before you preview the animation, look at Figure 6-5 (don't peek at 6-6) and see if you can figure out the anagrams. (Award yourself three red stars for each correct answer!) The answers—with their opacity set to zero—are concealed in the spaces between the lines of text.

OK, time's up. To see the finished Flash animation, visit the Little Red Books site at www.littleredbooks.com/anagrams.htm. Figure 6-6 reveals the completed anagrams.

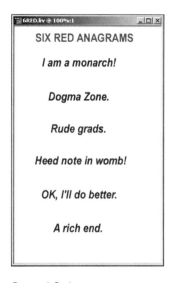

Figure 6-5: Anagrams.

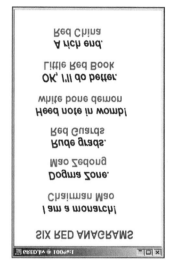

Figure 6-6: The answers revealed.

Since I'm often forced to eat my own words, that should be enough irony to hold us over until dinner.

The Anagram Timeline

Figure 6-7 shows a portion of the timeline for Six Red Anagrams—the complete animation consists of 12 lines of animated text. Staggering the initial opacity keyframes on the timeline makes each line fade in sequentially. I saved time by setting the Opacity attribute for all of the text objects at once. I did this by holding down the SHIFT key and clicking each of the text objects in turn to select them all. Then I clicked the Opacity attribute for just the first line ("Chairman Mao"), and LiveMotion automatically set keyframes for all the remaining objects. I then made manual adjustments to the individual keyframes to achieve the sequential fade-in effect.

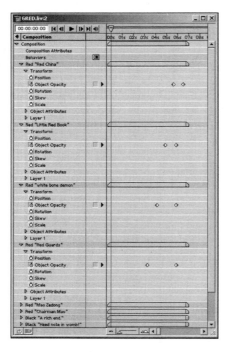

Figure 6-7: Staggered keyframes.

I could have made the text zoom across the canvas and spin, but that would have been both unnecessary and distracting. The composition has just enough visual motion to keep the viewer focused on what's most important—the text.

White Bone
Demon

Once you've animated an object, you can select it, copy it, and paste the animation to another object via Edit • Paste Object Animation. Be resolute and use this trick to keep all counterrevolutionaries in their place.

Putting Mao in Motion

One of LiveMotion's neatest features is the Break Apart Text command, found on the Object menu. This command allows you to place a line of text in a composition and break each letter into a separate object that can then be transformed independently. Without this feature, the process of animating text objects would be enormously tedious, as it is for those Flash running dogs.

Let's put this feature to use in a new animation called *Mao in Motion*. We'll cheat a teensy bit here by including a bitmap image of the Chairman.

Before we jump into the nuts and bolts, however, let's preview the animation's four main segments, shown in Figure 6-8. Although it spans 51 frames at a rate of 12 frames per second (fps), it weighs in at just under 4K.[4] In panel 1, we have the name *MAO* in red and an image of the Chairman. In panel 2, the letters *TION* slide in from the right to form a new word, *MAOTION* (that's literally Mao in motion). In panel 3, the word *LIVE* slides in from the left, as the *A* in *MAOTION* rises to meet *DOBE*, which slides down from the top. In panel 4, the image of Mao fades out while the word *LIVE* begins to drop down beside *MOTION*, giving us *ADOBE LIVEMOTION*. Since the letters *A*, *M*, and *O*, are in red, the connection between the Chairman and the software continues to echo after the animation ends. A nice touch. You can view the finished Flash animation at www.littleredbooks.com/adobe.htm.

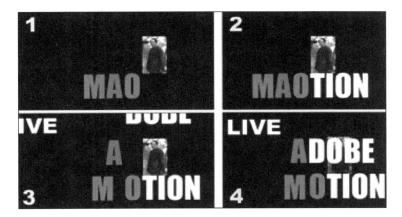

Figure 6-8: Gang of Four panels from Mao in Motion.

---

[4] Exported to Flash, the animation will load in 1.64 seconds when viewed on a 28.8 kbps modem. At 56 kbps, the animation will load at the lightning rate of 0.80 seconds. To learn how LiveMotion helps you manage and control animation size, refer to Chapter 8.

Creating Mao in Motion

Now let's re-create the animation. We'll leave out the image and focus on the type.

Place the Text

1. Start a new composition and size it at 450 x 225, at the default frame rate of 12 fps. Press CTRL-S and name the file maotion.liv.

2. Use the Paint Bucket tool to set the composition background color to black. Then, in the Color palette, change the foreground fill color from black to red.

3. Choose the Type tool and click inside the composition to bring up the Type dialog box. Select the typeface Verdana from the drop-down list. (If you don't have Verdana on your system, use an equally hefty specimen, such as Arial Black.) Choose Bold for the type's style (located in a drop-down menu to the right of the Font list), and size the type at 72 points. Click in the text entry area and type "MAO" (all caps), and click OK. (Note that Red MAO appears in the Timeline's hierarchy list. (If the Timeline isn't open, press CTRL-T.)

4. To position the text, enter the *X* and *Y* coordinates in the Transform palette as 88 and 122, respectively. Press ENTER.

5. The word *MAO* should still be selected in the composition. From the Object menu, choose Break Apart Text. Your composition should look like Figure 6-9. Notice that each letter has its own bounding box and is named automatically in the Timeline. Glance at the Timeline's hierarchy and you'll find that the object Red MAO has been replaced by the three individual letters as independent objects (Figure 6-10).

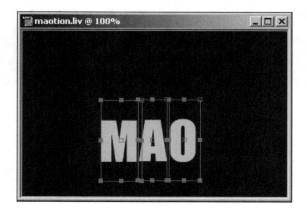

Figure 6-9: Text object after being broken apart.

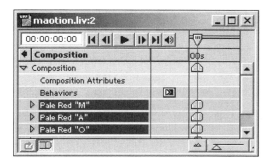

Figure 6-10: Three separate objects in the Timeline.

6. Now we'll add the other text objects and situate them *outside* the composition so they'll be hidden until needed. Maximize the composition window so you can view the gray area surrounding it and then, using the Selection arrow, click anywhere in the gray area outside the composition to deselect *MAO*. Using the Type tool, click in the lower right corner of the composition and type "ION" (all caps). You'll notice that LiveMotion's Type Tool dialog box remembers the last text you entered, as well as its characteristics. You need only replace *MAO* with *ION*, leaving the font and type size as is. Click OK.

7. *ION* is currently selected in the composition. Change the text object's color to white in the Color palette. (If *ION* is overlapping *MAO,* drag it away to the right.)

8. Now we'll add some guides so we can place the text precisely. From the View menu, choose the Show Rulers option. Place your cursor anywhere inside the horizontal ruler and click and hold the mouse button while dragging a guide onto the composition. Align it with the top of the letters in *MAO* (Figure 6-11).

Figure 6-11: Guidelines help keep unruly objects aligned.

Click and drag a second horizontal guide and position it just below the letters. With the Selection arrow, drag *ION* between the two guides, moving it just *outside* the composition. (When you do so, you'll no longer see the letters, only the bounding box. When you need to select the text again, you'll highlight it in the Timeline's object hierarchy list.)

9. Select the Type tool and click in the upper left corner of the composition window. Type the word "LIVE", and set the size to 48 points. Click OK. Set the object's coordinates in the Transform palette to $X = 11$ and $Y = 17$. Drag two horizontal guides for the top and bottom of the letters. (Align the guides with the letters, not the bounding box.) In the Transform palette, change the coordinates to $X = -147$ and $Y = 17$ to place the object just outside the composition.

10. With the Type tool, click in the upper right corner of the composition and type the letters "DOBE." Set the size to 72 points, click OK, and set the coordinates in the Transform palette to $X = 226$ and $Y = -15$. Drag two vertical guides from the ruler and place them at the outer edges of the letters "E" and "D". Change the coordinates in the Transform palette to $X = 228$ and $Y = -76$, and press ENTER.

11. Press CTRL-S to save your work.

Now all the actors are in position and ready to rock. Conjure up the Timeline (CTRL-T) and resize it so that it can be viewed along with the Composition window.

Animate the Text

1. In the Timeline, drag the Composition marker to 04s to set the duration for the animation. This sets the duration for the objects as well, but their durations can be changed when necessary.

2. From the Timeline's object hierarchy, select White ION. Drag its duration bar to 04s, set the CTM to 01s, and click the twisty next to the object to expand the attributes. Click the Transform twisty and the Position stopwatch to insert the initial keyframe at 01s, and then drag the CTM to 02s. Any manipulations to *ION* will be animated from the initial keyframe at 01s to the second keyframe at 02s. Pause and praise Mao Zedong for leading us to victory.

3. In the composition, select ION and drag it into the composition, using the guidelines as a track. If it rebels, beat it down forcefully. Move it until it joins MAO and forms the word

MAOTION. You can then drag the current time marker (CTM) back and forth to quickly preview the movement.

4. In the object hierarchy list, select Red A and drag the CTM midway between 02s and 03s. Expand its attributes and set a Position keyframe. Move the CTM to a point just before 03s. With the red A selected in the composition, change its *Y* coordinate to 45 in the Transform palette. This should position the letter up against the guideline.

White Bone Demon

After working with an object in the object hierarchy list, remember to click its twisty to collapse the Properties list—that way you'll be able to keep the Timeline from extending beyond view.

5. In the object hierarchy list, select White LIVE and move the CTM midway between 02s and 03s. Expand its attributes and set a Position keyframe. Move the CTM to a point just before 03s. With LIVE selected in the composition, change its *X* coordinate to 13 in the Transform palette. Again, you can "scrub" the CTM to preview your progress.

6. Now, select White DOBE in the object hierarchy list and move the CTM midway between 02s and 03s. Expand its attributes and set a Position keyframe, then move the CTM to a point just before 03s. (You can align it with the LIVE object's keyframe.) With DOBE selected in the composition, change its *Y* coordinate to 46.

7. In the object hierarchy list, select Red M and move the CTM to 03s. Expand its attributes and set a Position keyframe. Move the CTM to a point just between 03s and 04s. With the red M selected in the composition, drag it to the right so that it forms the word MOTION. Let your heart swell with pride.

8. Finally, select White LIVE in the object hierarchy list and move the CTM midway between 03s and 04s. Expand its attributes and set a Position keyframe. Move the CTM to 04s. With LIVE selected in the composition, change its *Y* coordinate to 146.

9. Press CTRL-S to save your work. Remember, no wind, no waves.

10. It's been a bit exhausting, but we're done! In the Toolbox, click the Preview Mode button and admire the animation.

We've created a couple of animations that have effectively subverted text by transforming just object opacity and position, but that's only the tip of the iceberg—imagine the possibilities with stretching, skewing, rotating, and deforming type. Even with the most radical effects, you follow the same basic path as in the previous exercise: set an initial attribute keyframe at the point in the Timeline where the transformation begins, drag the CTM to the point where it will end, and then manipulate the object in the composition however you wish.

Wao Mao!

Figure 6-12 shows a frame from a Flash animation titled Wao Mao, which transforms the opacity and position of the three letters, scales and rotates them, and makes them interact in a rhythmic Maoist dance. You can view the animation at www.littleredbooks.com/waomao.htm and then download the original file (waomao.liv), open it in LiveMotion, dissect it, and jazz it up.

Figure 6-12: Wao Mao *(7K Flash animation).*

For added visual drama, I selected a vector arrow shape from the Library palette and stretched it into a spear. It enters the composition at what I call the *climox* (the climax of motion) and strikes at the letters, propelling them into the distance like a pack of cowardly imperialists.

Use the original LiveMotion file to study the positioning of the keyframes in the Timeline and see exactly how the movement is accomplished. Once you've seen how it works, try swapping keyframes to reverse object movement. Drag keyframes closer to speed up the action, and spread them apart to slow the motion down. Delete keyframes and create your own. Let a hundred keyframes bloom! Use the file as fertile seeds for an entirely new animation!

When viewed on the Web, *Wao Mao* loops continuously. Usually, my preference is for nonlooping animations. I like to use Flash as a teaser, leaving the viewer wanting more and—hopefully—forcing him or her to return to the page for additional viewings and deeper indoctrination. Why the exception here? I think the loop adds a hypnotic quality to the motion.

Check it out and see if you agree.

To make your own animation loop, select Composition in the Timeline's object hierarchy list and depress the loop button in the lower left corner of the Timeline. To preview the animation, click the Preview Mode button in the Toolbox or—better yet—view it in your browser by choosing File • Preview In.

Preview mode is a clunky tool (my least favorite LiveMotion feature) and will not always offer an accurate presentation of the final result. It's really acceptable for only the simplest animations. Even though it takes a moment longer, I recommend previewing your work in a browser.

Type in LiveMotion—if it's unadorned with styles and textures—has the distinct advantage that it exports as vectors, not bulky bitmaps, and so your text animation files will be remarkably small. For example, had I chosen three bitmap images for *Wao Mao* and manipulated them in the same precise fashion, the file would have ballooned. As it is now, it's a speedy 7K.

White Bone
Demon

Remember that the "Big 5" transformations under the Transform heading in the Timeline are generally the most efficient to animate, and they require the addition of roughly 6 bytes per attribute per frame of animation for each object. So animating the size, opacity, and skew of the letter *A* over ten frames would add something like 180 bytes to your animation, while animating *Apple Macintosh* would add 2.5K. That's why, if you were to animate the tracking of *Apple Macintosh* over 2 seconds at 20 fps, you'd see 10K added to your .swf file (plus whatever space is needed for the letters themselves).

Although you may be tempted to do fancy things that will transform text into a bitmap (for example, adding drop shadows from the Styles palette), don't underestimate the power of plain proletarian vector type. It can be used to produce powerful, animated propaganda that loads quickly in a browser, even at slower connection speeds.

More Text Worship

Another unique advantage of using LiveMotion for text effects is that it is simple to animate type characteristics such as font, orientation, and leading without tweening these changes over time. For example, from the Timeline, you can set a stopwatch for Text under Object Attributes and thereby have the text change at different times in the animation. You could have the word *Animate* become *Infiltrate* at 2 seconds; then, at 3 seconds, the word could transform into *Dominate*.

Let's try an example.

1. Start a new composition.

2. From the Window menu, choose Reset to Defaults to return all of the palettes to their original position and set the current fill color to black.

3. Select the Type tool, click in the center of the composition, and type the word "motion."

4. In the Timeline, drag the Composition duration bar to 02s.

5. Click the twisty next to Black motion, and then click the twisty for Object Attributes. Click the Text stopwatch.

6. Drag the CTM to 02s.

7. Press V to call up the Selection tool, and double-click the text object in the composition. Change the word to "potion."

8. Click the Play button and preview the change.

White Bone Demon

Not every object attribute shows up by default on the Timeline. (Adobe did this deliberately to conserve space, as LiveMotion can animate more than a hundred attributes.) Certain hidden attributes are revealed only after you make changes to the object in the composition or from a palette. For example, once you adjust a text object's tracking in the Properties palette, Text Tracking will appear in the Timeline's Object Attributes list. The same holds true for leading.

You can add other transformations on the Timeline as desired. Using this technique, you can create a classic countdown animation ("10 . . . 9 . . . 8 . . .") and countless others.

LiveMotion also lets you animate the tracking and leading of words without breaking them apart into uneditable shapes, as Macromedia Flash does. For example, Figure 6-13 shows a paragraph featuring lyrics from a catchy Red Guard song. Figure 6-14 depicts the same paragraph after the leading and tracking have been tweened. The text stretches out, expanding to nearly twice its original size. To do this, I set a stopwatch for the Replace attribute (Figure 6-15), which allows you to replace text, and then adjusted the leading and tracking in the Transform palette. I was also able to make a significant change in the text.

Figure 6-13: Catchy Red Guard song.

Figure 6-14: Catchy Red Guard song with leading and tracking tweened.

Animating attributes in the manner just described can result in fairly bulky Flash files, through no fault of LiveMotion's. This is due to the nature of the Flash player, which must animate each character separately. Thus, be judicious when animating Text Size, Text Aspect Ratio, and Shape Resize from the object hierarchy list.

White Bone Demon

Avoid tweening certain type attributes if you wish to maintain a respectable file size. For example, beware of animating the Text Size attribute, since a new Type object will be stored on every frame, fattening the file like a corrupt landlord's lackey. Instead, scale the object via its bounding box.

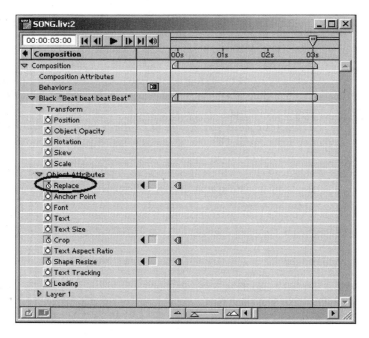

Figure 6-15: The Replace attribute.

Last Anagram Before Toll

On the book's companion Web site you can view the animated anagram depicted in Figure 6-16. When you click on the button at the bottom, it changes color and triggers the letters in the phrase "An immoral loving ache" to drift down slowly, intermingle, and reform into a new sentence. The phrase remains at the bottom of the screen, and clicking the button a second time has no effect. The page must be refreshed in order for the Flash to replay.

After viewing the animation at www.littleredbooks.com/ache.htm, download the original LiveMotion file (ache.zip) at www.littleredbooks.com/download. Your assignment is to edit this animation so that the button continuously triggers the falling text. You must make the animation loop so the letters return to their original position and wait for the viewer to act—just as in *Nerd Descending a Staircase* (Chapter 5). If you need a guide and didn't download nerd.liv, you can do so at www.littleredbooks.com/download. You can open up both files in LiveMotion and use *Nerd* as your guide.

Figure 6-16: Flash in progress.

Famous[5] Lost Words

It's a well-established fact that Chairman Mao had an eye—as well as other anatomical parts—for the ladies. To be sure, his private life makes ex-President William Jefferson Clinton's Oval Office romps seem about as licentious as a game of mah-jongg. What is not widely known—and is more shocking still—is the fact that Mao was also a flagrant punster.

Among his trusted inner circle, he would occasionally unleash a torrent of groaners that had them heading for the gates at Zhongnanhai. Alas, only a few examples of Maoist wordplay have been smuggled out of China, and most of them are lost in translation. One surviving specimen, however, was related to me recently by China scholar Ming Burroughs at his retreat in Connecticut. It goes something like this. . .

---

[5] Note that the name "Mao" is contained in this word *famous*.

Mao was strolling along the beach at Tsingtao, accompanied by his burly bodyguard, Hu Dek Pao.
It was a fine spring day, yet the Yellow Sea had deposited large clumps of rotting seaweed in the sand.

Hu Dek suddenly clutched his nose and cried, "*Oh, what a stench!*"

Mao paused to look at the tangled mass of weeds that littered the shore like gleaming barbed wire.

"It's a shame," mused the Chairman wistfully. "You just can't find good *kelp* nowadays."

Even on his deathbed, the Chairman maintained his sense of humor, planting a joke in the last line of his will:

"Take my wife . . . *please!*"

Unfortunately, after he passed from LiveMotion Leader to Inert Icon, the Central Committee missed the joke and *did.*

Original Mao button designed by Wai Hang Mi.[1]

---

[1] In 1964, 10,000 aluminum copies of this button were reportedly produced by the Beijing Red Smile Badge Factory. Shortly after they appeared, Lin Biao publicly denounced the button, saying, "Chairman's Chin Tu Fat." The artist, Wai Hang Mi, was forced to wear the unsold stock—pinned to his flesh. Extremely rare today, the original button is believed to be responsible for the insidious "Smile Cult" that spread around the world.

7

MAO BUTTONS, GUERRILLA ROLLOVERS, AND MASS MOVEMENT:
Correct Behaviors and Interactive Elements

The Mao button (Smi Li) is one of the defining symbols of the Great Cultural Revolution and the Cult of Mao. At the very least, it's the loudest fashion statement ever made.

In his excellent and exhaustive study, *Badges of Chairman Mao Zedong*, Bill Bishop estimates that, in 1969, more than 90 percent of the Chinese people wore them. Furthermore, as many as *5 billion* badges may have been manufactured since the first button rolled off the presses sometime in the summer of 1966.

According to Bishop, Maoist loyalty was measured by these questions: "First, can you dance the loyalty dance? Second, do you have a 'little red book'? Can you recite it? Third, do you wear a Chairman Mao badge?"[2]

Today, the question of one's loyalty should be amended as follows:

Do you have Derek Pell's Little Red Book? *Does your Web site have a Mao button?*

Complete the exercises in this chapter and your answer to the latter will be a resounding "You bet!"

---

[2] *Badges of Chairman Mao Zedong* (1996) by Bill Bishop (www.cnd.org/CR/old/maobadge/index.html).

Do-It-Yourself Mao Buttons

Since you can't be a SoMo[3] in the People's Animation Army without a Mao button, let's make a pair and then create a rollover with them.

1. Download the file mao1.zip from this book's companion Web site (www.littleredbooks.com/download/mao1.zip), and extract it to a folder on your desktop.

2. Start a new composition; size it at 500 x 300, and set the frame rate to 10. Since we're going to export our rollover to a page with images and JavaScript, be sure to select AutoLayout in the Export drop-down list in the Composition Settings dialog box. Choose GIF as the export format (File • Export Settings). I'll discuss the ins and outs of Export in Chapter 8.

3. Press CTRL-S to save the file, and name it "2maos.liv."

4. Set the fill color to black. (If the Color palette is hidden, press F6 to display it.)

5. From the Toolbox, choose the Paint Bucket and click inside the composition window.

6. Press V to switch to the Selection tool, and choose File • Place. Locate the downloaded mao1.gif file on your computer, and double-click its icon. By default, LiveMotion positions the image in the center of the composition. Select and drag it to the upper left corner.

    NOTE *Since we'll be using this image again later in the chapter, drag and drop it into the Library palette and name it "Mao Button."*

7. With the image selected in the composition, press CTRL-D to place a duplicate on top of the original. Drag the copy below the original Mao button so that both are visible.

    NOTE *As you drag the copy across the original, the transparent GIF's rectangular black border becomes visible. For this exercise it's not a concern since the images won't overlap. But if you wanted to hide the border so that the button could overlap another object, you would choose Active Matte from the Alpha Channel drop-down list in the Properties palette.*

---

[3] Soldier of Motion. SoMo should not be confused with the Japanese form of wrestling.

8. With the duplicate still selected, hold down the SHIFT key and click on the top button to select it as well.

9. Choose Object • Align • Horizontal Centers to center the objects precisely. (This may not impress you now, but just wait until you need to crack down on a recalcitrant gang of objects spread all over your composition.) Click in an empty area of the composition to deselect the buttons.

10. Press CTRL-T to summon the mighty Timeline. In the hierarchy list, select the top button, press ENTER, and name it "top." In the same manner, name the other button "bottom." (With just two objects in our composition, naming them may seem unnecessary, but it's a good habit to develop—especially for the complex animations you'll soon be creating.)

Our two lonely Mao buttons look like they're eager to interact. That means it's time for rollover action! Happily, LiveMotion makes it easy to create rollover effects, whether you aim to create a Flash (.swf) animation or a more traditional Web page made from images, HTML, and JavaScript. In either format, LiveMotion creates all of the coding for you. All you have to do is export the file to an HTML page and you're ready to roll.

Making Mao Kowtow: Creating the Rollover

Now let's make the Chairman bow to our will.

Create the First Rollover

1. In the composition, select the top Mao button.

2. Press F11 to display the Rollover palette.

3. Notice that Mao is highlighted in the default Normal[4] state. At the bottom of the palette, click the New Rollover State icon (Figure 7-1) to create an Over state. (*States* allow LiveMotion to display different versions of an object under particular circumstances. The Over state of an object appears

Figure 7-1: Clicking the New Rollover State icon on the Rollover palette.

---

[4] The term is, of course, relative.

when a user moves his or her mouse over that object—pretty intuitive, eh?)

4. We want the Chairman to react when the mouse moves over him, so we'll change his appearance in the Over state we just created. Choose Window • Distort to define the Over state. (Note that this action leaves other states, such as the Normal state, untouched.)

5. In the Distort palette (Figure 7-2), select Twirl from the drop-down list. Change the default setting for Turns to –29 (either type the number or drag the slider bar), and press ENTER to initiate the effect.

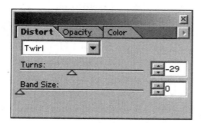

Figure 7-2: The Distort palette.

6. Press Q on your keyboard to enter Preview mode, and move your mouse over the button (Figure 7-3). Not bad, but don't throw your rice just yet. Press Q again to return to Edit mode.

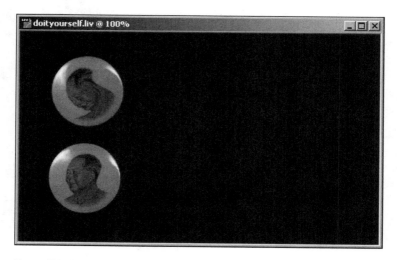

Figure 7-3: Mao's over.

Make Both Buttons React

To make both buttons react to a mouseover, we could select the bottom button and repeat the preceding steps, but, in Mao's words, "*Wai Du Ha Wok?*"

1. Select the top button and press CTRL-C to copy it. Select the bottom button and choose Edit • Paste Style. Press CTRL-S to save.

2. Press Q again and test both buttons.

    Pretty cool . . . . Now both buttons bow. But for them to really interact we need to flip the bottom button horizontally.

3. Select the bottom button and choose Object • Transform • Flip Horizontal to force Mao to face the opposite direction.

4. Save the file and preview it.

5. Stand and take a bow.

Correct Behaviors

"The Communist Party . . . cannot deal with patriarchal behaviors."
—Chairman Mao

We've got our rollover working, but how do we make the buttons do something like link to a Web site? Luckily, LiveMotion makes this task easy: We simply add a *behavior*. Behaviors are events or actions that are triggered at a specific point in the Timeline or when a user interacts with a button. For example, by attaching rollover behaviors to the Mao buttons, we can make them do our bidding. Let's make the top button link to the Little Red Books Web site.

Link to a Web Site

1. Select the top Mao button in the composition.

2. In the Rollover palette, click the New Rollover State button to create a Down state. (A Down state defines what happens when a mouse clicks *down* on a button object.)

3. Click the Edit Behaviors button on the Rollovers palette.

4. From the Add Behavior drop-down list, choose Go To URL (Figure 7-4).

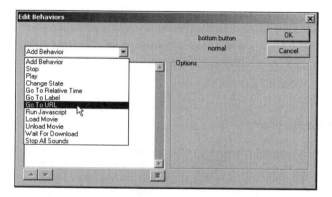

Figure 7-4: Choosing the Go To URL behavior.

5. In the URL text entry box, type "http://www.littleredbooks. com" and click OK. Press CTRL-S to save your file.

To test the link, connect to the Web and, in LiveMotion, choose File • Preview In. Select your default browser. Once the page has loaded, click the top Mao button and visit the Little Red Books site.

Like a lively Red Guard march through the streets of Beijing, behaviors add deep, interactive dimensions to the animation landscape. You can access LiveMotion's built-in series of preset behaviors (Figure 7-5) by clicking the Timeline's Behaviors icon (Figure 7-6). Advanced users can add custom JavaScript commands by choosing Run JavaScript from the Edit Behaviors dialog box. We'll investigate advanced behaviors in Chapter 9.

A lively Red Guard march.

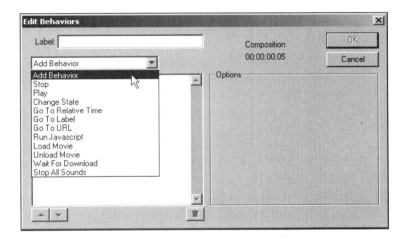

Figure 7-5: Displaying the preset behaviors.

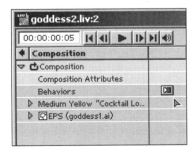

Figure 7-6: Clicking the Timeline's Behaviors icon.

Red Romance

Let's try a new rollover effect, using three objects and a behavior: a heart image that triggers an animation of two kissing silhouettes.

Create the Silhouettes

1. Download maosil.zip from www.littleredbooks.com/download/maosil.zip.

2. Start a new blank white composition and size it at 400 x 300, with the default frame rate.

3. Press CTRL-S and name the file "romance.liv."

4. Be sure the fill color is set to black.

5. Choose View • Show Rulers and drag a guide from the horizontal ruler, positioning it at the vertical 1-inch mark.

6. Choose File • Place, and import maosil.gif. Drag and drop it into the People's Library palette and name it "Mao Silhouette." We'll work with a copy from the Library, so delete the original from the composition.

7. Set the Library palette view to Name, select Mao Silhouette, and drag the image into the composition, aligning the top of Mao's head with the guide.

8. In the Transform palette, set his coordinates to $X = 203$, $Y = 100$.

9. In the Library palette, locate Profile Woman and drag it into the composition. In the Transform palette, set her coordinates to $X = 69$, $Y = 100$.

10. In the Timeline, highlight Black Geometric, press ENTER, and name it "Woman." Click OK.

11. With Woman selected in the composition, choose Object • Transform • Flip Horizontal. (Remember, Flip Horizontal flips the object horizontally so that it faces the opposite direction.)

Add the Heart

Now the lovebirds are facing each other. Can't you just feel the erotic tension in the air? Well, maybe not—so let's add some.

1. Return to the Library palette, locate Heart, and drag it into the composition.

2. In the Transform palette, change the heart's width to 65 and its height to 75. Align the base of the heart with the guide and position it between the couple (Figure 7-7).

Figure 7-7: Maoist lovebirds.

3. With the heart selected, choose a bright red in the Color palette.

4. In the Timeline, highlight Red Geometric, press ENTER, and name it "Heart." Click OK.

The stage is now set for some ribald dating behavior (rated PG, of course).

Animate the Kiss

Let's make our couple kiss when a mouse moves over the heart.

1. In the Timeline, drag the composition's duration bar to 01s.

2. Select Woman in the object list and click her twisty to reveal the attributes. Click the Transform twisty and its stopwatch icon.

3. Set the CTM to 01s.

4. In the Transform palette, set Woman's coordinates to $X = 109$, $Y = 100$.

5. Drag the CTM back and forth to preview the kiss.

6. In the Edit Behaviors dialog box, select Stop from the Add Behaviors drop-down list. Under Options, the default Target will be Composition, which is what we want. The Stop behavior literally stops the animation in its tracks. The target indicates the object we want the behavior to affect—in this case, it indicates where the movement occurs—the composition.

7. Select Play from the Add Behaviors drop-down list. (Again, the Target listed under Options should be Composition.) Click OK. We have now set a state that, when triggered, will play the animation.

Trigger the Animation

Now we'll set the heart to trigger the animation.

1. With the heart selected in the composition, press F11 to display the Rollover palette.

2. Click the New Rollover button. Select the Over state, and click the Edit Behaviors button.

3. Choose Play from the Add Behaviors drop-down list, and choose Composition from the Target drop-down list.

4. Click OK.

The Timeline should resemble Figure 7-8. Press CTRL-S to save your work; test the animation by choosing File • Preview In and select your browser.

Always remember, when the revolution bogs down, you can add a dash of romance to spice it up.

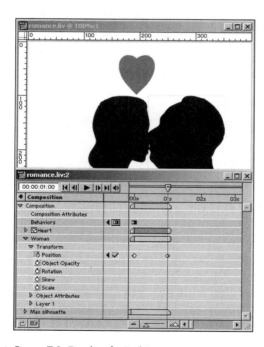

Figure 7-8: Timeline for Red Romance.

Remembrance of Nerd's Past

You'll recall that in Chapter 5 I discussed the animation *Nerd Descending a Staircase*. If you didn't have an opportunity to download the original LiveMotion file (nerd.zip), please do so now at www.littleredbooks.com/download/nerd.zip.

Figure 7-9 shows portions of the Rollover palette and the Timeline. (To view the complete Timeline, open nerd.liv in LiveMotion; you can also view the finished Flash animation online at www.littleredbooks.com/nerd.htm.) It illustrates how I used behaviors to create the Play button that triggers the animation. The Play button has a Play behavior attached to its Down state; the composition, which is set to loop, has a separate Stop behavior (which I labeled "wait") set at 00s. Thus, the animation "waits" for action by the viewer, since the Stop behavior freezes it at 00s. Clicking the Play button triggers the Play behavior (which has the composition as its target), sending the nerd down the stairs. As soon as the animation loops back to the first frame (00s), the Stop ("wait") behavior kicks in so that the Play button must again be clicked to launch the action.

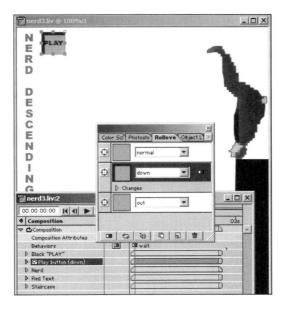

Figure 7-9: Nerd behaviors.

The simple examples we've explored in this chapter should give you a hint of just how powerful LiveMotion's behaviors are. Chapter 9 will look at more advanced behaviors.

"Export Chairman Mao's Revolutionary Line!"

8

IMPORTING AND EXPORTING THE REVOLUTION: Working with Layered Photoshop Files and Exporting Flash

One of LiveMotion's *big* advantages is its ability to import Adobe Photoshop and Illustrator files *and* maintain their layers. You can create a layered image in either Illustrator or Photoshop, prepare it for eventual animation, and take comfort in the fact that—with one click of the mouse—you can convert each layer into a separate object that can then be edited on the LiveMotion Timeline. You can edit these layers-turned-objects by applying layer effects and styles and altering their optimization settings. (You cannot, however, edit vector points, erase pixels, and so on.) This feature alone makes the program worth every capitalist coin you've invested.

This chapter focuses on Photoshop (.psd) files, but bear in mind that you can do the same with your Illustrator creations.

Importing and Manipulating Files

The process couldn't be simpler: Either drag your layered Photoshop file directly into a LiveMotion composition, or use the File • Place command. Once it's imported, choosing Objects • Convert Layers Into • Objects lets you manipulate the layers as objects. (You could animate the imported object as a whole, but we want to deal with each layer separately in this chapter.)

Here are the other options available under Convert Layers Into:

- **Group of Objects.** Automatically places the newly converted objects into a single group.
- **Sequence.** Converts layers into separate frames; all the frames form a single object in the Timeline.
- **Sequence with Background.** Converts layers into separate frames, but with the background on a separate layer.

If that's not radical enough for you, consider this: Once you've imported a Photoshop or Illustrator file and converted its layers to objects, you can adjust each object's brightness, contrast, saturation, and tint—all via the Adjust palette. You can also invert an object's colors or posterize[1] it. Further, you can emboss, bevel, ripple, and perform all manner of transformations to objects in the 3D palette. You'll also find a nice selection of native Photoshop filters that you can apply to objects under Object • Filters.

But wait, I've saved the best for last—the Edit Original command! This feature lets you select your layer-turned-object and launch Photoshop or Illustrator to edit it. Make your changes, save them, and—presto!—the changes appear instantly in LiveMotion.

White Bone
Demon

When jumping back to Photoshop, beware of adding a layer to the .psd file, since upon your return you'll discover that LiveMotion has inserted a whole new copy of the composite file. To get around this, merge the new layer into the old one (using Merge Down in Photoshop) before you save and return to LiveMotion.

The LiveMotion User Guide and Help system must be reeducated! In order for the Edit Original command to work, you might have to manually place a shortcut to Photoshop in LiveMotion's Helpers/Graphics Editors subfolder. The shortcut to Illustrator should go in the Helpers/Vector Editors subfolder. These shortcuts should be created automatically upon installation, but often they aren't. If your Edit Original command is dimmed, manually placing the shortcuts will solve the problem.

---

[1] Change the number of colors in an image; e.g., reducing the number of colors in a continuous-tone photo flattens the colors and makes it appear painted.

The Writing on the Wall: Using Layers to Animate an Autograph

Recently, Comrade Miggs Burroughs assigned me the task of transforming painter Elise Black's signature into a Flash animation for her Web site's splash page. The signature was to appear on a black background and was to flow naturally, as if being signed by an invisible hand. There was no time to incorporate a video clip. The work was to be a basic Flash animation.

This was the first time I had encountered such a task, so I wasn't sure exactly how to proceed. It seemed the solution was to use a mask in LiveMotion so I could trace each line segment and reveal it gradually. I proceeded to build the animation using a mask, only to discover that the final result looked choppy and unnatural. No amount of tweaking seemed to work.

A mini-Maoist brainstorm sent me back to the drawing board: What would happen if I used Photoshop's Lasso tool to divide up the signature? Working in Photoshop with a traced bitmap of the signature, I inverted its color to get white lines on black. Then, using the Lasso tool, I selected segments of each letter (Figure 8-1) and pasted them into a new Photoshop file. When I was finished assembling the fragments, I had a .psd file that comprised 12 layers.

Figure 8-1: Selection made with the Lasso tool.

Figure 8-2 shows the layers that form the signature. Note that layers 11 and 12 (representing the lower segments of the letter *k*) have been turned off and are not visible. By first turning off all of the layers and then manually turning each one on in succession, I was able to view a "rough" of the animation and easily spot flaws. (Figure 8-3 shows a misalignment where the letters "B" and "l" are joined, as well as a "chip" in the line segment. I easily repaired the blemishes using the Paintbrush and Eraser tools.)

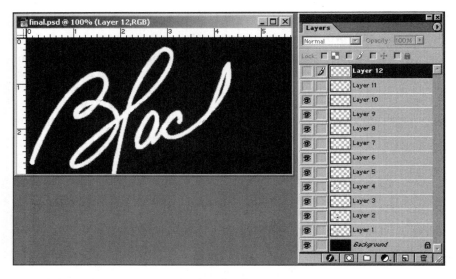

Figure 8-2: Line segments on separate Photoshop layers.

Figure 8-3: Purging flawed line segments.

Next, I dropped the finished Photoshop file into LiveMotion and converted the layers to objects (Figure 8-4). I then animated each object's opacity in the Timeline and adjusted the keyframes of each line segment so they would fade in sequentially, making the signature appear to write itself. You can view the final Flash animation at www.eliseblack.com.

The Little Red Exercise Book

Let's look at another example of how Photoshop and LiveMotion struggle together as comrades in arms. In May 1968, a crude, mimeographed pamphlet appeared on the streets of Beijing. *The Little Red Exercise Book*[2] was released in a limited edition, published by the People's Animation Army Lonely Hearts Club Band (Figure 8-5). The pamphlet (featuring cover girl Jiang Qing) was edited by one "Pinyin Tin" and was distributed on the streets by Red Guard "volunteers." In a matter of days, the booklet leaped to the top of

---

[2] Future printings appeared under the title *Mao Tu Fat Exercise Book*.

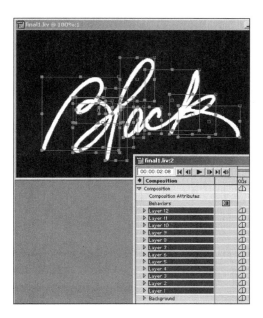

Figure 8-4: Photoshop layers converted to objects in LiveMotion.

Figure 8-5: Cover of rare Maoist pamphlet.

the *New China Times* bestseller list, where it remained throughout the Cultural Revolution.

I'm pleased to report that—until now—this extremely rare edition has never been seen outside the People's Republic of China. As a reader of this book, you should consider yourself quite fortunate, for you're getting *two* Little Red Books in one.

I must confess, however, that when I first got my hands on a copy I was disappointed that it was only 16 pages long—far too slender a volume for me to cash in on the exercise book craze. But I immediately saw the book's potential as a motion graphic—and the rest is history.

Figure 8-6: Face east and strike a fierce, anti-imperialist stance. Chant "The East is Red and so am I!".

Figure 8-7: On balls of feet, pivot 180 degrees. Read aloud Quotations of Chairman Mao Zedong.

Figure 8-8: Shut book. Tap right foot three times in honor of san da fa bao.[3]

Figure 8-9: Place book on head. Swing arms to left. Swing arms to right. Chant "Let's go Red Guards, Fight! Fight! Fight!". Do not drop book!

---

[3] The three magic weapons. Mao believed that the communist revolution succeeded because the party relied on "the United Front, armed struggle, and *The Little Red Book of Adobe LiveMotion.*"

Figure 8-10: Pivot 90 degrees to defend the Party against reactionary snakes and spies.

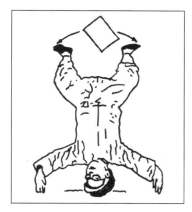

Figure 8-11: Stand on head. Juggle Little Red Book. Read between the loins.[4]

Figure 8-12: With revolutionary zeal, throw book at nearest capitalist roader.

Figure 8-13: Oops! You hit Comrade Hua Guofeng. Sentence yourself to ten years of hard labor.

Then again, maybe not. But be that as it may, I've included the book's central text and illustrations here (Figures 8-6 through 8-13). After you've had a chance to practice the exercises (and commit the text to memory), we'll use the images to illustrate LiveMotion's Place Sequence command.

---

[4] This last line is a loose translation provided by a cab driver in Brooklyn.

Placing the *Exercise Book* Images as a Sequence

LiveMotion lets you import a range of separate image files as a sequence to be used in an animation. This is a great timesaving feature that you should definitely take advantage of.

To import a series of files as a sequence, make sure you name them sequentially—for example, File1, File2, and so on. I saved the eight images from the *Exercise Book* into a folder on my desktop (Figure 8-14).

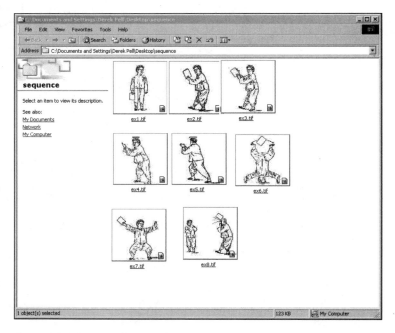

Figure 8-14: Sequentially named TIFs awaiting import into LiveMotion.

I then launched a new composition in LiveMotion, chose File • Place Sequence, opened the folder containing the files, highlighted the first image (ex1.tif), and clicked Open.

When a series of numbered files is imported as a sequence in this way, LiveMotion keeps the files in their proper numeric order, places the sequence as a single object in the center of the composition, and automatically inserts start and end keyframes for the Object Time attribute (Figure 8-15). (Object Time marks the duration of the sequence from first image to last. You can decrease the speed at which a sequence plays by dragging the duration bar to extend it, moving the end keyframe ahead in the Timeline; if you move the two keyframes closer together, the sequence will speed

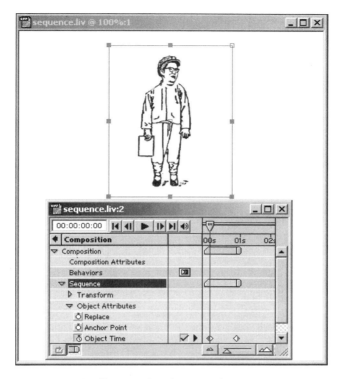

Figure 8-15: The sequence placed as a single LiveMotion object.

up.) The sequence can then be previewed via the Timeline's play-back controls. If the animation is not to your satisfaction, you can extend a sequence's duration bar by dragging it or by reposition-ing the keyframes to speed up or slow down the animation. (The closer the keyframes, the faster the sequence.)

NOTE *To turn the exercise images into a fluid Flash cartoon, I would have had to add a dozen drawings to portray the figure's intermediate positions. Being lazy, I exported the sequence as a quick GIF animation (via the Export palette) to be used on my Web site to keep away the crows.*

If you want to add a sequence of images to an existing anima-tion at a specific point in the Timeline, drag the CTM to the position where you want the images to appear *before* choosing Place Sequence.

Defeating Low Bandwidth by Exporting Small Files!

Perhaps, in some distant utopian future, all communards will be blessed with swift and sure Internet connections and a single omnipotent browser (Figure 8-16). A smiling Chairman will man the Gates of Heavenly Bandwidth, eagerly bowing and serving the masses. LiveMotion cadres armed with this *Little Red Book* (the 34th printing) will wave it high beneath a mighty Maoist sun. We will all sing "The East Is Red" and march through cyberspace united.

Figure 8-16: The browser of the future.

"Defeat all bourgeois hacker claques!" we'll shout.

Yes, it sounds like I've been dipping into the opium again.

For now, unfortunately, anarchy and chaos reign on this vision of a bright proletarian parade. Instead of speed and cyber-beams, we have lethargic phone lines and creaky 56K modems that croak and crawl and deadbeat dialups and ISPs that gouge the masses like fast-buck feudalist landlords. We sputter, stumble, and crash through the digital universe, crying out for tech support.

Because we are realists, we keep the masses—our audience—in mind. We remain vigilant, ever conscious of the fact that the size of our animations must be kept under the control of the dicta-torship of the proletariat. When exported, we want our files to load quickly in different warring browsers.

White Bone
Demon

When you export an animation as a Flash file, be wary of adding layers to a vector object, as it will export as a bitmap. You can defeat this demon by making changes to a layer's Object Layer opacity. That way, the vector format remains unchanged.

THE PEOPLE'S GALLERY

ART FOR MAO'S SAKE

Greetings Foreign Guests!

Step forward (no leaping) into Great People's Gallery Exhibit of Liberated Socialist People's Art by Comrade Norman Conquest and (his handler) Comrade Derek Pell. All art is subject to change without notice and may not be touched. Violators will be opposed and punished for their crimes. Enjoy yourself!

—THE PEOPLE'S COMMITTEE ON EXHIBITIONS OF CORRECT SOCIALIST PEOPLE'S ART IN THE SERVICE OF OUR GLORIOUS LEADER, CHAIRMAN MAO ZEDONG

The Little Chairman

Early portrait of the Great Helmsman. It was said that, even as an infant, Chairman Mao appeared "wise beyond his ears." [sic]

Chairman Mao Presides Over the Grand Opening of Red Lobster (Hunan, 1964)

This festive and friendly military restaurant was constructed at great sacrifice to serve the leaders of the great People's Animation Army. So festive and friendly, Red Lobster has today spread throughout China, and is the country's Number One Socialist Fast Food for Thought chain.

Zelda Zedong

Rare portrait of Chairman Mao's sister. Known to her friend as "Zee Zee," she volunteered in the great Revolutionary Struggle. Her contributions to the Long March included serving dinners for 35,000, and heroic chores such as cleaning up after her brother. Upon her successful arrival in Dawei, she committed suicide.

Mao Action Figure Set

Highly collectible communist party favor. Informally known as "Gang of Three," the limited edition set was distributed to only the first 800,000 lucky visitors to the Little Red Books Web site (www.littleredbooks.com). Manufactured to strict Oppose Cult of Personality Communist Doll Standards, the lifelike action figurines feature a simulated naugahyde-embalmed inner shell to keep out foreign invaders. Each is fully poseable, articulated, and comes with detachable head.

Unauthorized Edition

A book of object lessons for wayward Maoists. See Chapter 3 for details.

Little Red Sex Book

Banned in Beijing, but still available under the counter at Great Wallmart.

Long Live Adobe LiveMotion!

Revolutionary parade celebrating the great advance in Flash animation as a result of the People's Timeline.

Little Red Book Funnies #1 (Class Struggle Comics, 1973)

Fun-filled People's commie book, interpreting the great work by Comrade Derek Pell. Characters include "Goofy" (US president); Mighty Mao; Bugs Bunny (Wen Ho Lee); and a billion others. Features connect-the-dot mushroom cloud, Taiwan dartboard, paper tiger cut-outs page, and more!

Red Guard Pep Rally (Flash)

Red Guard cheerleaders perform for a thousand Maos.

Layout for Red Goddess (Flash)

You're not in Kansas anymore. See Chapter 9.

Early cover design

This lovely artwork was produced in Photoshop, but was deemed "too romantic" by the publisher.

Red Goddess Lights

Discontinued after revisionists added warning label: MAOISM MAY BE HAZARDESS TO YOUR WEALTH.

Little Red Book with Hook

Artist book-object by Norman Conquest. This convenient edition will hang just about anywhere.

Banner ad for Little Red Books

Designed according to the strict specifications of Mao Zedong Thought, the image strikes a balance between good taste and revolutionary showmanship.

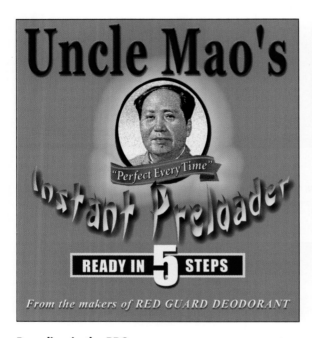

Branding in the PRC

Fast food for Flash. See Chapter 11.

"Defeat stinks!"

—CHAIRMAN MAO

Sign for popular Chinese restaurant chain

Billions served, naturally.

"To spy or not to spy . . . is not the question. Rather, who's to spy on your spies' counterspies? Now there's the rub!"

—CHAIRMAN MAO

Popular "Hard Sell" Red Book ad campaign

Incorporates the motto of the modern People's Animation Army.

Portrait of Young Mao as Flash Cadet in Adobe Motion patrol

The People's Layout with Flash added

A rebel-burst explodes in the visitor's face, driving home the message.

Flash Web layout with gong and Mao buttons

Sound and interactive elements combine forces in this motion layout.

Animated entrance to Hypertut 2000

Animated type elements and lighting effects create a dramatic entrance to this experimental Web site.

Flash animation for Storm Films

Using Photoshop, sky and lightning were added to the author's original photo. The layered image was then imported into LiveMotion and animated.

Animated splash screen for Dingbat Magazine

Evidence that this popular American Web site has been infiltrated.

"To rebel is good. To merchandise is even better."

Revolutionary Vectors vs. Reactionary Bitmaps

There will be times when we must sacrifice a big, beautiful bitmap of the Chairman because using it would require the People to wait ten minutes for it to appear on their screens. (Not even Mao's mother would wait that long for an animation to load.)

One way we can keep file sizes down is by using vectors instead of bitmaps. The top image in Figure 8-17 shows a 17K bitmap created when I applied a fancy LiveMotion style to a vector "Red Goddess" logo created in Illustrator. The file size becomes problematic if I try to animate the logo and import some other objects. The bottom screen in the figure shows the same logo in its original vector state. Without the fancy style, it weighs in at under 4K and still looks pretty good.

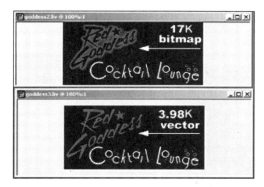

Figure 8-17: Bitmap file size versus vector file size.

Keeping Tabs on Your Objects

When preparing animations, keep track of the size of your objects —especially when using more than a few—to keep the overall file size (shown in the lower left corner of LiveMotion's status bar) down. To get a report on the sizes of different elements in your file, choose View • Active Export Preview. To see if a specific object will export as a vector or as a bitmap, select the object in the composition and choose View • Active Export Preview. In the status bar at the bottom of the LiveMotion window, you'll see either a pen icon (vector) or picture icon (bitmap). The byte size of the selected object is also indicated.

NOTE *When finished, be sure to uncheck Active Export Preview. Otherwise, the program takes a noticeable performance hit.*

From Tai Chi to Sci-Fi: Using the Report Function

Now I'll show you how to use LiveMotion's report feature and Export palette to export animations swiftly and effectively.

Launch your browser and visit www.littleredbooks.com/alien. htm. There you can preview my Flash animation *Birth of an Alien, 2001* (Figure 8-18). For this discussion, we'll look only at how to use the report function. You'll get to work with the original .liv file in Chapter 10.

This project began innocently enough with an antique doll my wife reluctantly let me play with. I placed it face down on my flatbed and scanned it into Photoshop. The results were pretty weird (Figure 8-19), but not weird enough for what I had in mind. After hours of experimenting with various plug-in filters and working with the trusty Clone tool, I had three versions of the doll that I wanted to combine in a Flash animation. I sandwiched two of the images on their own layers and saved the third image separately.

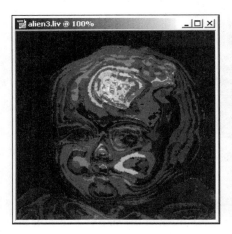 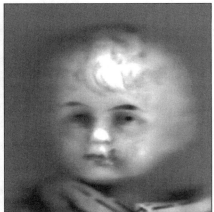

Figure 8-18: Birth of an Alien, 2001.   *Figure 8-19: Original scan of doll.*

Dragging the layered .psd file onto a blank LiveMotion composition, I converted the two layers into objects. In the Timeline, I animated the top object's opacity so that the bottom object's visibility weaves in and out. Lost in the throes of creation, I neglected to consider the size of the ultimate file. At this point, the animation was already 9+ seconds long. Always aware that I may have to leave something on the cutting room floor (or, to paraphrase the British writer John Cowper Powys, to kill my darlings), I figured it was time to run an interim export report—one of LiveMotion's valuable features. To use it, you must first preview your work in a browser (File • Preview In). When the browser launches, Live-Motion inserts an Export Report link just below the animation. Click the link to view the report.

Figure 8-20 shows a partial display of the stats for *Alien*, including total file size (38.77K), the duration in frames (117), the frame rate (12 fps), and approximate download times at three different modem speeds. The Download Streaming table gives a frame-by-frame breakdown of byte size and load times. At the bottom of the report (not shown in the figure) is a Resources table listing each object in the animation and its format, size, and quality settings.

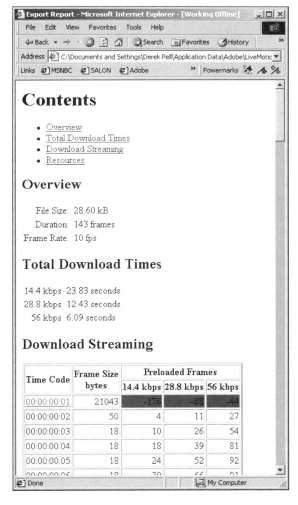

Figure 8-20: An export report.

Since I still had another object to add to the mix, the report showed signs of danger—a load time of 8.25 seconds with a fast 56K modem.

I began a serious round of self-criticism: Did I need to use bitmaps, or should I trace them and convert them to vectors? Could the quality settings be adjusted downward? Should I remove frames to cut down the animation's duration? Or should I resize the entire composition?

As you can see, export reports can be crucial to the design process, prompting many important questions. In the case of *Alien,* I opted to "go with the flow" and fiddle with quality and size settings later.

Back in LiveMotion, I used the File • Place command to import the third image. I then resized it and animated its opacity, position, and rotation.

Another preview, another report. The animation now weighed in at 48.39K and consumed 171 frames, with the download time on a 56K modem up to 10.3 seconds. It was way too fat of a capitalist roader.

Using the Export Palette

It was time to do some tweaking in the Export palette and create the final Flash file. To summon the palette from the menu, I chose Window • Export. Figure 8-21 shows the palette with the initial settings for *Alien.*

The SWF Flash format is the default export setting. Additional format options available from the drop-down list are Photoshop, GIF, JPEG, PNG-Indexed, and PNG-Truecolor[5].

Figure 8-21: The Export palette.

The default setting for objects is JPEG, which offers the best combination of quality and compression for photographs and images with graduated tones. For images with flat colors, drawings, and logos, you'll get the best results with the GIF format. The handy slider bars change the overall quality and opacity resolution; the two pull-down menus below them let you set the MP3 data rate and the

---

[5] PNG format, although gaining in popularity, is still not widely used. A plug-in is required for older browsers to view it.

animation frame rate. Finally, the last drop-down menu lets you specify whether to export the entire document or a single object.

Optimizing *Alien*

To reduce *Alien's* file size, I first reduced the frame rate to 10 fps, but the Export Report showed minimal results—the file size was still a hefty 47.91K.

Although the Quality setting was a conservative 40, I knew I could decrease it further as my images were blotchy and sharpness was not a factor, so I changed the Quality to 19. I also lowered the Opacity Resolution setting to 4. (Opacity resolution is the level of precision with which LiveMotion follows the edge of an image containing transparency. Such images have a mask layer that defines where the transparency exists. The more detailed the mask, the finer the edges and the larger the image.)

Running another preview and report, I discovered that the file size had dropped dramatically. It was now a manageable 28.6K, and the images still looked fine.

But what if you wanted to apply different quality settings to various objects in your composition? For example, let's say you import ten photographs, nine of which look fine with a JPEG quality setting of 30. The tenth photo, however, looks as if it was dragged through the mud by a band of hyperactive Red Guards. It needs a quality setting of 50. Rather than requiring you to choose to degrade the one image or to bloat the file by setting the quality too high for the others, LiveMotion offers *per-object compression* so that you can apply custom settings to individual objects. To add a custom compression setting, select an image and choose Object from the bottom of the Export palette. Then click the Create Object Settings button in the lower right portion of the palette to apply the settings only to the selected object. If you later specify settings when Document is selected in the Export palette, the settings apply only to the images without object-specific settings.

Animate or Bust: Using Layers and Report to Animate Effectively

In the next example, Photoshop and LiveMotion join forces to animate a bust of Mao. You can view the finished Flash animation—*Double Take*—at www.littleredbooks.com/double.htm.

How Did I Do It?

Photoshop's cool 3D Transform filter enabled me to take a flat, two-dimensional image of a bust of Mao and turn it into a three-dimensional object. I was then able to rotate it, producing two views of the object. Each view, plus the black background, was on a separate layer. I saved the native .psd file to my desktop and then dragged it into a blank LiveMotion composition (Figure 8-22).

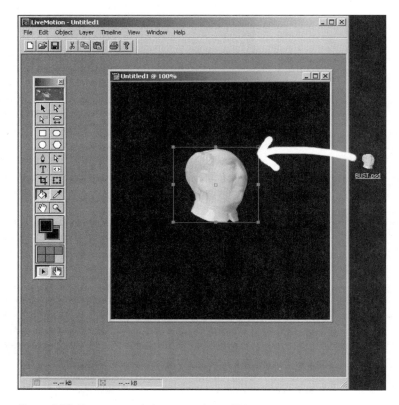

Figure 8-22: Dragging and dropping a bust of Mao.

I then converted the three layers into objects (the background and the two bust images), as shown in Figures 8-23 and 8-24; added a rectangle and the text *Double Take* (shown in Figure 8-27); and extended the composition duration bar to 03s.

I selected the top object in the Timeline and changed its opacity to 0 (Figure 8-25), which revealed the layer below (Figure 8-26).

Next I reset the top object's opacity back to 100. In Figure 8-27, you see the four contiguous keyframes that result in the appearance of the head turning. The opacity has to change abruptly, otherwise an extended fade would reveal both images and destroy the illusion.

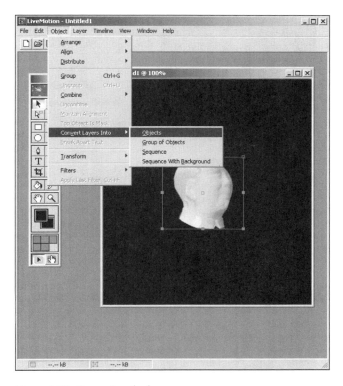

Figure 8-23: Converting the layers.

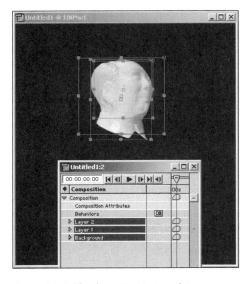

Figure 8-24: The three LiveMotion objects.

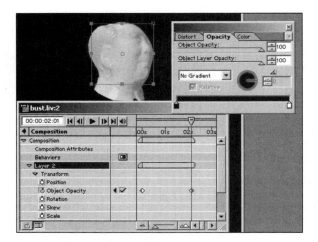

Figure 8-25: Animating the top layer's opacity.

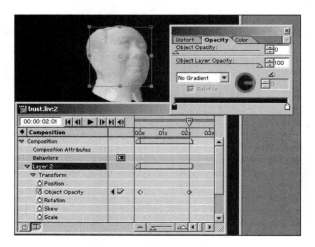

Figure 8-26: The underlying view of Mao's head.

After importing the lovely lingerie model, I animated her position (Figure 8-28) so that she enters the composition, flies past Mao, and stops at the bottom of the frame. There's a brief pause, then Mao does a double take.

Once I'd previewed the animation in my browser, I checked the export report to find that the file was a compact 12.59K—no further tweaking was necessary. I then exported the animation as Flash and later inserted the .swf file directly into Dreamweaver, where I saved the final HTML page.

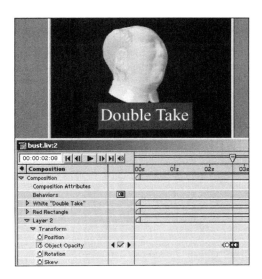

Figure 8-27: Adding keyframes.

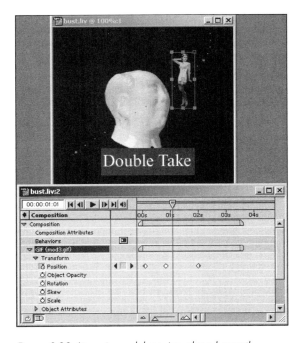

Figure 8-28: Lingerie model moving along her path.

Exporting Objects and Layouts to HTML

In addition to producing fierce Flash animations, LiveMotion is a great place to design and create layouts or page elements for the Web (see Figure 8-29). You'll find the program's page-creation capabilities particularly handy when, for example, you decide you'd like to preserve some artwork and interactivity from an .swf composition for use in an HTML page for users without the Flash plug-in.

Figure 8-29: Sample layout in LiveMotion.

Whether you're creating a single Web page or a hundred, you can design everything right in LiveMotion and export it directly to an HTML file. The process is straightforward. Once you've finished designing your layout in the composition, choose the format (GIF, JPEG, or PNG) and quality settings for the images from the Export palette. Then, from the File menu, select Export to launch the AutoLayout dialog box. Select a folder to store your work, type a name for the file (the default setting is HTML), and click Save.

Behind the scenes, LiveMotion produces all of the HTML[6] and JavaScript code, creates a table and *slices* the scene (divides the scene by placing any objects that are grouped or are touching in the same image file) to preserve your design, and exports all of the graphics to a new folder named Images.

---

[6] The simple layout for *Red Detachment of Women* fills ten pages of code!

When starting a new composition for export to the Web, remember to choose AutoLayout and Make HTML in the Composition Settings dialog box.

Be forewarned, though, that HTML has plenty of limitations. Further, since LiveMotion cannot export layered DHTML and preserves only a fraction of SWF animation and interactivity when exporting to sliced formats, you should design with a sliced layout in mind. Also, avoid overlapping slices; otherwise a demonic error message rears its ugly head: *"Could not export due to overlapping objects."*

Once you've generated an HTML page in LiveMotion, you can open it directly in a Web design program like Dreamweaver or GoLive for further tweaking and additions. You can also launch Preview In and then view the code in your favorite browser and copy and paste it into another HTML page in, say, Dreamweaver.

Saving Face with Batch Replace

One of LiveMotion's wickedest features is its Batch Replace command. It acts like a stealth bomber striking enemy HTML tags. It's swift and sure and can save you precious design time, as well as face.

Batch Replace allows you to replace tagged text in an HTML page with graphics created in LiveMotion. If you've had some experience with HTML code, it's a piece of cake. If you haven't gone underground before, here's your chance to be a brave guerrilla fighter and wage some batch warfare.

The following is a brief example of how to replace HTML text with graphic buttons. Remember, this barely scratches the surface of the Batch Replace function, as it offers a variety of applications and capabilities.

Replacing HTML with Graphic Buttons

First, I created some text in Dreamweaver—*press, bash, stomp, smash*—each separated by a hard return. Working in Source Code mode, I tagged each word with the <h1> headline tag. Figure 8-30 shows Dreamweaver in Split View mode, showing the HTML code at the top and the page with text to be replaced at the bottom.

After saving the file, I opened LiveMotion and created a beveled red button. I added the text *Beat Me* to the button, grouped the two objects (Object • Group), and saved the file. I then went to the Web palette (Window • Web) and, from the Replace drop-down list, selected the <h1> tag as the target for annihilation (Figure 8-31). Now I was ready to launch my surprise attack on the unsuspecting text in Dreamweaver.

Figure 8-30: Editing the HTML tags.

Figure 8-31: The Web palette's Replace menu.

To replace the text, I chose File • Batch Replace HTML (Figure 8-32) and, in the Open dialog box, located my HTML file. Returning to Dreamweaver, I opened the file to view the results shown in Figure 8-33.

A direct hit!

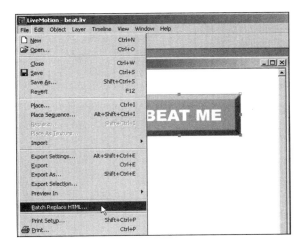

Figure 8-32: Choosing Batch Replace HTML.

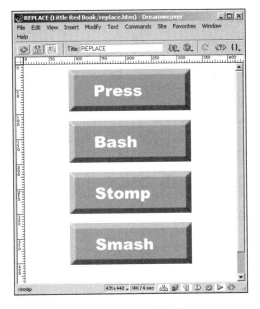

Figure 8-33: Mission accomplished.

"When at bottom, steal top secrets." —CHAIRMAN MAO

9

THE PEOPLE'S WAR OF INDEPENDENTS: Conquering Time-Independent Groups

Roll up your sleeves, Comrades . . . . Prepare to invade foreign territory and make great advances in the field of espionage.

We will plant the seeds of World Wide Web revolution behind enemy Timelines. We will set up nested spies in time-independent groups. We will infiltrate and subvert motion graphics with Marxist TIGs. We will subdue and defeat slow-loading capitalist roader freeloader Flash animations with Proletarian Preloaders.

Workers of the Web, unite!

Meet Me After Midnight at the Red Goddess . . .

One foot inside the Red Goddess and you know you're not in Kansas anymore.

It's the most mysterious cyberbar on the Internet, as dark and musty as the wings of an abandoned off-Broadway theater. It's an opium den-cum-clandestine cocktail lounge. Retro noir. It's Orson Welles meets Fu Manchu, starring Charlie Chan in drag. A password whispered through a slot in the door gains you access. You enter a narrow bamboo corridor with tattered red lanterns overhead, their skin etched with the alluring curves of two Chinese characters: "Girl Power."

Neon entrance to the Red Goddess.

You find yourself moving through a maze of scarred glass mirrors haunted by sparks of candlelight. The air thickens with incense, cheap perfume, and day-old noodles as you follow a laddered path to a room the size of an armory. There, in the center, stands a circular bar with a pink-tented dome, surrounded by a train of wooden booths resembling *wagons-lits*—each shrouded with a silken scrim on which the occupants' silhouettes appear. Smoke drifts languorously, rising in curls toward a ceiling fan that spins on borrowed time.

As vivid as the Red Goddess may seem, for a time it existed only in my imagination. Long hours of labor, sweat, and imagination brought forth this virtual den of iniquity—a nest of wanton women and chain-smoking spies—into my Little Red Books Web site—a place where communards slouch and skulk, swapping LiveMotion secrets. Check it out at www.littleredbooks.com/goddess.htm.

In the next section we'll work on an animated Red Goddess sign while learning the basics of time-independent groups.

The Time-Independent Group

A *time-independent group* (TIG) is a single animated object or group of objects that runs within (yet remains independent of) the main animation. Remember the French Marxist Regis Debray's book *Revolution in the Revolution?* Well, a TIG is an animation *in* an animation.

That may sound like a Zen koan, but TIGs can actually make your work in LiveMotion easier. Let's say you're animating a scene in which a robot moves about a room and pauses before a clock on the wall. The hands of the clock spin rapidly. The robot exits while the clock continues to spin, and then some text slides into the scene and the robot returns. By using a TIG, you can make the clock hands loop continuously without affecting the main animation. As an independent object, the clock gets its own Timeline and can have its attributes altered outside the clutter of the main animation Timeline.[1]

Creating an Animation with a Time-Independent Group

We'll create an animated Red Goddess logo (Figure 9-1), using a TIG in which a pair of provocative female eyes fade in and out in a continuous loop.[2] The main animation will feature a Maoist power fist and some humorous text that jumps into the composition.

Figure 9-1: Red Chinese spy nest.

---

[1] One advantage Macromedia Flash has over LiveMotion is the ability to divide an animation into separate scenes. I hope Adobe incorporates this feature into a future version, but for now we must work with TIGS or make separate animations that we later combine.

[2] The images of the eyes and fist in this exercise are part of a cool dingbat font set, Hong's 2 Dings Normal (created by Hong Li), which I've converted into GIFs. See Appendix B for some great font resources.

Create the Composition and a TIG for the Eyes

1. Download spynest.zip from www.littleredbooks.com/ download/spynest.zip, and unzip the files to a project folder on your desktop. Resave spynest.liv with a unique name so you'll still have the original .liv file if you need it.

2. Choose Window • Export, and make sure the format is SWF and the compression method is JPEG in the Export palette. Set the Quality slider bar to 56 and the Frame Rate to 10 fps.

3. Press CTRL-T to access the Timeline. Drag both the composition and "logo" duration bars to 05s.

4. Drag the CTM to 02s. Import eyes.gif (using File • Place), and place the image in the center of the composition. Choose Object • Arrange • Send to Back, and click and drag the eyes behind the Red Goddess logo. Position the right eye just above the second "d" in the word *Goddess* (Figure 9-2).

Figure 9-2: Placement of the eyes.

5. "GIF (eyes.gif)" should now be highlighted in the Timeline list. To create the TIG, choose Timeline • Make Time Independent Group (Figure 9-3). This action pops the eyes in front of the logo. To fix this, choose Object • Arrange • Send to Back again.

Make the Eyes Fade In and Out

1. The Timeline list now displays the new Group of 1 Objects. Double-click this item to call up its TIG Timeline (Figure 9-4), and click Group of 1 Objects in the list to select it. Move both the CTM and the group's duration bar to 01:06.

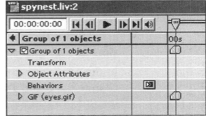

Figure 9-3: Creating the TIG.   Figure 9-4: The TIG Timeline.

2. Set the CTM back to 00, click the twisties beside GIF and Transform, and click the Object Opacity stopwatch. In the Opacity palette, set the Object Opacity to 0 (not the Object Layer Opacity!). Now move the CTM to 00:07 and set the Object Opacity to 100. Finally, move the CTM to 01:03 and set the Object Opacity back to 0 (Figure 9-5).

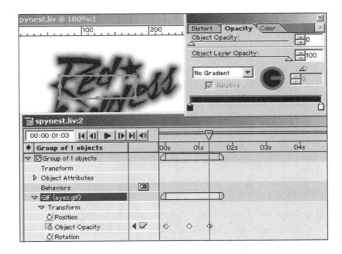

Figure 9-5: Setting the opacity of the eyes.

3. To make the eyes' TIG loop continuously, click Group of 1 Objects in the list and click the Loop button in the bottom left corner of the Timeline. Return to the main composition by clicking the black arrow to the left of the group's title bar.

4. Click the composition title bar to make it active, and press Q to preview the TIG in action. (Press Q again to return to Edit mode.)

Add the Red Guard Power Fist

1. Drag to resize the composition window so about an inch of gray border surrounds it. Then import the file fist.gif (included in the spynest.zip file).

2. In the Transform palette, change the *X* and *Y* coordinates to 73 and 359, respectively, and press ENTER to place the power fist just outside the composition (Figure 9-6). We'll have it enter the animation from here.

3. With the fist highlighted in the Timeline list, press ENTER and name it "FIST." Click OK.

4. Click the twisties beside FIST and Transform, and click the Position stopwatch.

5. In the Timeline, drag the CTM to 01:00. Then, in the Transform palette, change the *Y* coordinate to 196 and press ENTER. Click the composition title bar to

Figure 9-6: Positioning the Maoist power fist.

make it the active window. Press Q to preview the animation. (As always, press Q again to stop.)

Add Text

1. Now we'll add a nice comic touch. Using the Type tool, click an empty area inside the composition to bring up the dialog box. Select a font of your choice, and size it at 24 points. (I used the typeface Wonton[3] for an appropriately wanton effect.) Set the text alignment to centered, and type the following:

```
Complimentary
Wen Ho Lee
Cocktail
```

Click OK.

---

[3] Created by Da Font Mafia.

2. To keep the text out of the path of the fist, reposition the text so that the "C" in *Complimentary* lines up below the second "d" in *Goddess*. Change the type color to anything you like.

3. Try adding the Red Goddess style[4] to the text. Select the Goddess logo in the composition, and press CTRL-C to copy it to the Clipboard. Now click the text to select it, and choose Edit • Paste Style. Pretty snazzy.

4. Now let's animate the text with a LiveMotion preset. Set the Library palette to Name View, and find and highlight "anim arc fade left" in the list. Click the Apply Style button. Figure 9-7 shows the animation style applied to the text.

Figure 9-7: Animation style applied to text.

5. Press CTRL-S to save the file, then preview it in your browser and run an export report.

Trim and Slim the Goddess

As sexy as she is, the Red Goddess has got to go on a strict Maoist diet. Although your stats may vary slightly from mine, when I turn on View • Active Export Preview she tips the scales at 40.12K. Can we knock off some dead weight? The biggest offender is the bitmap logo (20K), but removing the layered style would ruin the effect of the eyes peering through a veil. The Quality setting is already low (56). Reducing the frame rate from 10 fps to 8 fps gets us to a flat 40K. That's no great shakes, although every little bit counts.

---

[4] Courtesy of Daniel Gray.

But does the type for the Wen Ho Lee joke really have to match the logo's style? It sure doesn't—*goodbye* style! To get rid of the style, select the text and then, in the Object Layers palette, delete the bottom two layers by selecting each and clicking the trash icon. Now, with the style gone, the text object is returned to its natural vector state and the file sheds some capitalist fat. The final result: a perfectly respectable 27.61K. But don't take my word for it—preview the Flash and then check the export report.

TIGs in the War of Independents: A Quick Quiz

The crass Flash animation in Figure 9-8, *Mao on Crass Warfare*, contains two looping GIF animations I downloaded from the Web: a revolving red star (which I duplicated via CTRL-D) and a moving tank that shoots.

In order to make the GIFs loop when exported to Flash, you must set the composition to loop via the button on the Timeline. But suppose that you wanted the second line of text to fade in and freeze yet keep the GIFs looping—what then?

Figure 9-8: Mao on Crass Warfare.

Yes, Comrades, you'd deploy People's Animation Army TIGs to save the day. In this case, you'd select the tank and make it a TIG; then select both stars and make them a TIG, too.

Figure 9-9 shows the two TIGs in the Composition list— note how neat and clean the Timeline looks. No mess, no *Confucius*. TIGs leave plenty of room for maneuvers.

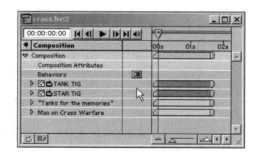

Figure 9-9: Crass Timeline with TIGs.

You can view the little 11K animation on this book's companion Web site at www.littleredbooks.com/crass.htm.

Thank you, Chairman Mao; you're the biggest, brightest TIG of all!

Banner Ads: "To Rebel Is Good, to Promote Is Even Better!"

I've made a mini-career out of promoting nonexistent products—everything from coin-operated paperbacks to lawn chairs made out of grass. I've pushed Red Guard Deodorant, Baudrillard's Simulacrum Cake, Foucault-Text, and Cheaties, to name but a few. Call it vapor-capitalism or virtual marketing, it's just Avenue Madness from someone reared in Westport, Connecticut, right in the shadow of Madison Avenue.

Ready-to-eat surreal.

Thus, it'll come as no surprise that while still at work writing this book, I decided to create an animated banner ad (Figure 9-10) to inspire advance orders for it. Heck, it was already being advertised on Amazon.com. Besides, I owed it to Mao's Marketeers.

Figure 9-10: Vanguard banner ad.

It struck me that the PRC flag was a prime candidate for animation—not only are flags in general the ultimate sales tool, hyping nationalism, patriotism, and nostalgia for days gone by, but the PRC flag in particular has nice, bright colors and a chorus line of stars.

As motivated as a man with a brand new Mao suit, I headed for Photoshop and prepared the artwork. I kept each element (type, stars, Mao, and colored background) on a separate layer and exported the file in native .psd format, ready to use some TIGs to make the image come alive.

Animating the Banner Ad

Placing the file in LiveMotion, I transformed the layers into objects, selected the four small stars, and made them into a TIG. Double-clicking Group of 4 Objects, I switched to the group's Timeline (Figure 9-11), where I animated the stars so they'd twinkle. Returning to the main Timeline, I worked on the image of Mao—animating the object's Position, Object Opacity, Skew, and Scale attributes (Figure 9-12).

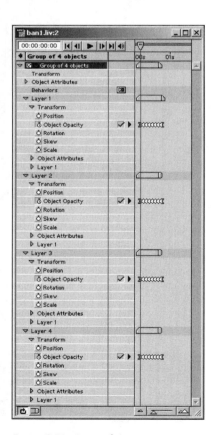

In preparation for the coup de grâce, I minimized LiveMotion and copied the URL address for the order page at Amazon. Then, returning to the Timeline, I selected all of the objects (including the background) by pressing CTRL-A. In the Web palette, I pasted (CTRL-V) the address into the URL box. Selecting all of the objects ensured that a click anywhere inside the animation would trigger the link.

I then exported the file as a Flash animation, embedded it in an HTML page, and uploaded it to the Web. Of course, I wisely saved my originalLiveMotion file for future editing. That way, when the book was

Figure 9-11: Gang of 4 stars.

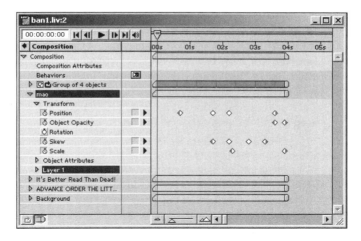

Figure 9-12: Mao's keyframes in the main Timeline.

published, I could delete the word *advance* and continue to run the ad. Remember to always save your original .liv files, since LiveMotion makes it easy to update them.

Now, Comrades, it's time to try your hands at creating your own animated banner ad. Go forth and market!

Ten Thousand Timelines to Chairman Mao

The genesis for this next animation was a work of experimental literature: Raymond Queneau's *One Hundred Thousand Billion Poems* (Figure 9-13). Queneau—a French writer and mathematician—

Figure 9-13: Raymond Queneau's Cent Mille Milliards de Poèmes (1961).

concocted ten sonnets, each line of which could replace, or be replaced by, its homologue in the other nine poems—thus yielding 10^5 possible combinations (a sonnet has 14 lines). I wanted to pay homage to Queneau's brilliant piece of "potential literature" via visual art and was inspired to try my first attempt at motion graphics—a GIF animation called *One Hundred Thousand Billion Women (give or take a few)*. Since I'd failed math in high school, I felt obligated to add the parenthetical qualifier.

I thought it would be fun to update the animation for this book and—thanks to LiveMotion—add an interactive dimension not possible with GIFs. Renamed *Red Heads*, the new Flash version (Figure 9-14) was assembled as follows:

I began with the images of six faces[5] that I cut into three sections. Starting with the foreheads, I scanned the six images into Photoshop and placed each on a separate layer. I followed the same procedure for the other two sections. When I was done, the eighteen scanned images were contained in three layered Photoshop files. (As you'll recall, I said I *thought* it would be fun.)

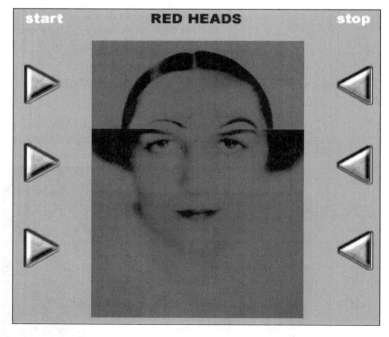

Figure 9-14: Red Heads, an interactive Flash animation (38K).

---

[5] I found them in a German fashion magazine, circa 1935.

I then fled to China.[6]

Rested and imbued with the spirit of the Great Helmsman, I imported the .psd files into LiveMotion as sequences and then made each sequence (heads, eyes, mouths) a TIG (Figure 9-15) that continuously cycled though each of the six images like a slot machine.

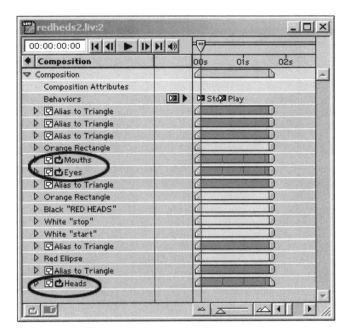

Figure 9-15: The three little TIGs.

I then created the Start and Stop buttons and applied behaviors to them, linking each button to the appropriate TIG. The user can now turn each section off and on at will and, as a result, potentially view 216 different women.

You can view the animation on the Web at www.littleredbooks.com/redheads.htm or download the original .liv file from www.littleredbooks.com/redheads.zip and pull it apart in preparation for working with advanced behaviors in Chapter 11.

---

[6] Bill Pollock, my publisher, had the CIA track me down, and I was extradited back to the States and forced to fulfill my contract.

Parting Head-Shot

One Flash tidbit before moving on to Chapter 10. When viewing Flash in your browser, did you know you can zoom in for super close-ups? Place your cursor on the area of the animation you want to enlarge, right-click, and choose Zoom In from the menu. Right-click again to zoom in closer.

Figure 9-16 shows a zoomed-in view of the *Red Heads* animation.

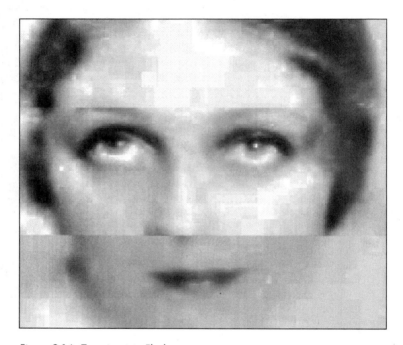

Figure 9-16: Zooming into Flash.

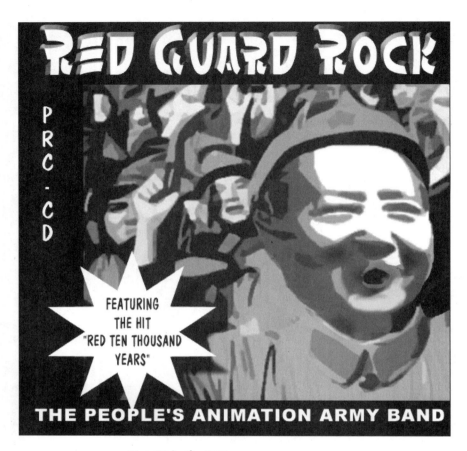

Hot CD in the PRC

When Red Guards rock, the heads will roll,
The motion revolution gonna blow your soul!
Our hearts are red, our book's red, too,
Capitalist lackeys'll be black 'n' blue!!
A thousand flowers bloom, red roses anew,
Yo, Chairman Mao, this bud's for you!
Papa ooh-Mao-Mao, Papa ooh-Mao-Mao,
Uh Papa ooh-Mao-Mao, Papa ooh-Mao-Mao,
Uh Papa-papa-papa ooooooh...[1]

---

[1] From *Red Ten Thousand Years.* Lyrics © 1969 by Hu Sung Mai-Dung.

10

THE GREAT WALL OF SOUND:
Adding Audio to
Flash Animations

Imagine a revolution without sound . . . .
No call to arms, no shot heard 'round the Web.
No chanted slogans, no revolutionary songs.
No catchy model operas like *Taking Tiger Mountain
by Strategy*. No marching bands, no May Day parades.
Rebel-rousing speeches unspoken, quiet riots in the streets.
Silent movies. MTV in mute mode.
No Acid wok!
Despite today's tin pan
bandwidth, the Web is wired
for sound. And it doesn't
take a weatherman to know
which way the wind blows.
The PC of the future will be
the TV. (Heck, some things
never change.) For now,
streaming audio and MP3
are the vanguard of this
nascent revolution. But a
Great Wall of Sound is coming soon.

If you use sound judiciously, it can enhance and add depth to your Web site. It can rivet an audience, or at least wake it up. It can set a mood, accentuate content, give drama to a presentation.

A full motion picture–style soundtrack isn't necessary to give the user a rich, interactive experience. In fact, blasting your visitors with too much sound, ill-suited music that can't be turned off, or a cacophony of effects like those in an old Spike Jones tune will have them pushing the panic button. Simple sounds attached to JavaScript rollovers, however, can provide an element of surprise or delight.

As I see it, the goal should be twofold: Hold visitors on your site for as long as you can, and keep them coming back for more.

LiveMotion does not stream sound—at least not yet—so long soundtracks, though possible, are difficult to achieve. (Future versions, I'm sure, will address this deficiency.) This chapter focuses on what LiveMotion does best—the creative application of small sound effects and sound clips.

Figure 10-1: The Sounds palette.

The Sounds Palette

LiveMotion's Sounds palette (Figure 10-1) has a selection of effects in AIFF format to get you started. You can add other popular formats to the library as well—WAV, SND, and AU—but not, however, MP3 (see White Bone Demon below).

White Bone Demon

LiveMotion lets you export in the MP3 format, but it will not import MP3 files. To import an MP3 file, you must first convert it to a supportable format such as WAV. You'll need third-party software for this task. One of the best conversion programs is SoundForge from Sonic Foundry. (For a complete list of audio resources, refer to Appendix B.)

The Sounds palette functions just as the Library, Textures, and Styles palettes do—that is, you add a sound object to your composition by either dragging and dropping, double-clicking its name in the palette list, or using the Insert Sound button. LiveMotion treats a sound clip as an object in the Timeline.

Adding sounds to your sound library is just as easy—just drop them directly onto the palette. As with LiveMotion's other libraries, you have a choice of views for the Sounds palette—Swatches,[2] Preview, and Name (the latter is depicted in Figure 10-1).

Undoubtedly, once you've played with Adobe's built-in collection of sound effects, you'll soon be craving more. Don't worry—there are literally thousands of free sounds and music clips available for download on the Web. (See Appendix B for a list of resources.) If your appetite craves even more sound bytes, you can always record your own and include them in your Flash animations.

Shake, Rattle, and Revolt: Sound Basics

To see how a sound object functions on a basic level, let's drag one into a blank composition.

1. First, make sure your speakers are turned on—a common oversight.

2. Start a new composition with the default settings in place.

3. In the Sounds palette, locate Bloop.aif and highlight it in the list.

4. Click the Play Sound button (located in the lower left corner of the palette) and preview the effect. Pretty neat, but it's just a bloop in the bucket.

5. Click the Insert Sound button and place the sound in the composition.

The composition still looks empty, but it's not. Bloop is hiding just below the surface like a little red submarine. To reveal Bloop, press CTRL-T and open the Timeline. There it is at the top of the list—"Bloop (event)"—with a speaker icon for easy ID. A light blue duration bar differentiates the sound object from other objects.

---

[2] I must confess that the point of viewing sound Swatches without a descriptive name eludes me, but then I'm not a sound technician.

Making Adjustments to Your Sounds

As with graphic objects, you can rename a sound by highlighting it in the Timeline and pressing ENTER. In this case the name is a perfect fit, so we'll leave it alone.

Click the twisties for Bloop and its Object Attributes to reveal Pan and Volume (Figure 10-2). The Pan attribute lets you switch the stereo signal between channels, and Volume, of course, lets you adjust the level higher or lower.

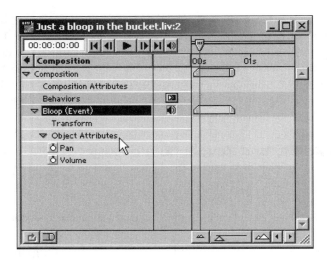

Figure 10-2: A Bloop in the Timeline.

To make more advanced adjustments to a sound object, select it in the Timeline and use the slider bars in the Properties palette (Figure 10-3). Here is a rundown of the different properties you can adjust:

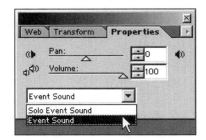

Figure 10-3: Properties palette.

• **Event Sound.** Downloads the entire sound before playing it and stores it in memory for repeated use.

• **Solo Event Sound.** Creates a flag that signals other instances of the same sound to stop playing so you don't get a dreaded echo effect when a button is clicked more than once.

Extending a Sound's Length

As indicated by the sound object's duration bar in Figure 10-2, Bloop plays for less than a second. Let's extend this limit by making the sound repeat.

1. Drag Bloop's duration bar to 03s. As you drag, note that the composition's duration bar extends to match the duration of the sound.

2. Click the Play button to preview the extended Bloop. The sound now repeats during its three-second lifespan. The four vertical lines in the duration bar mark where the sound will repeat (Figure 10-4).

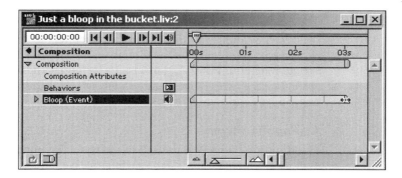

Figure 10-4: Extending the duration of the sound.

Alternatively, you can loop Bloop by highlighting it in the list and clicking the Loop button. The sound will then loop until the final frame of the animation is reached. In contrast, manually dragging the sound's duration bar lets you set precisely where the sound stops.

More Sound Adjustments

Here are some more operations you can perform on sound objects:

*   Reposition a sound object within an animation
*   Shorten a sound object if it plays for too long
*   Add sound to a TIG by dragging a sound object into the independent group's Timeline window.
*   Loop a sound throughout a Flash animation by making it a TIG in the manner described in Chapter 9.

Now that you've completed Bloop camp, you're ready for combat.

White Bone Demon

In order to loop a sound object, you must upgrade LiveMotion to version 1.0.2. Using the initial release (version 1.0) results in mysterious gaps between loops. Rumor has it the original code is haunted by the ghost of Rosemary Woods.[3]

Let the Nerd Be Heard: Adding a Repeat Effect

We'll start by adding a sorely needed sound effect to *Nerd Descending a Staircase,* the animation from Chapter 5. Even though I could watch this guy going downstairs for hours, the animation would be a lot better if we could actually *hear* his head hitting each step. So let's add some thumps.

Adding the Thump

LiveMotion's library of sounds didn't have the thump I was looking for, so I spent an hour or so surfing the Web in search of the perfect WAV. I sampled hundreds of boings, bangs, plunks, cracks, and splats until my head felt like it was trapped in a Looney Tune.

Suddenly—like music to my ears—I heard what I'd been searching for.

A pristine thump so perfect that it put to shame all the common thumps I'd previously endured.

So download nerd_thump.wav for free[4] from www.littleredbooks. com/download/nerd_thump.zip, and download the original *Nerd* LiveMotion file from www.littleredbooks.com/download/nerd.zip.

Once you've extracted the files to a folder on your desktop, launch LiveMotion and open nerd.liv. Now let's get down to business.

1. Grab nerd_thump.wav and drag it into the Sounds palette.

2. Accept the default name and click OK to close the dialog box.

3. Preview the sound using the palette's Play button.

---

[3] Richard Nixon's personal secretary, believed responsible for having erased 18 minutes of criminal conversations from a critical White House tape during the Watergate investigation.

[4] Is this book a bargain or what?

4. Press CTRL-T to bring forth *Nerd's* Timeline.

5. With the CTM set at 00s, click the button to the right of the Play control and advance through the animation one frame at a time. (You can also drag the CTM marker, if you prefer). Stop when you reach the frame where the nerd's head touches the second step.

6. With nerd_thump highlighted in the Sounds palette, click the Apply Sound button. The Timeline list now features "nerd_ thump (Event)," as shown in Figure 10-5.

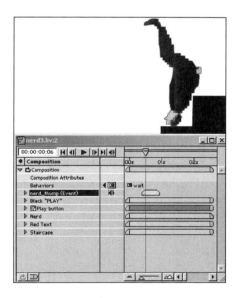

Figure 10-5: First thump.

7. Repeat Step 6 to insert the sound for all five steps.

8. Press CTRL-S to save the file. Your Timeline should have the same Zen-like symmetry as the one depicted in Figure10-6.

9. In the Export palette, change the format from the default JPEG to Indexed (this format reduces the number of colors, giving you a more efficient export), and set the Color slider bar to 42, Web Adaptive (Web Adaptive shifts image colors to Web-safe[5] colors). Now preview the results in your browser (File • Preview In).

---

[5] The 216 colors that all major platforms (Windows, Mac, Unix . . .) have in common.

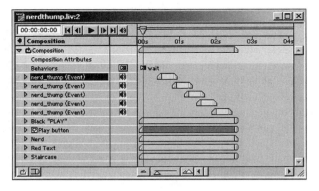

Figure 10-6: Staggered thumps in the finished Timeline.

10. Choose File • Export to generate the Flash file and you're done. Raise the Red flag in Victory and rock around the wok.

Using Preview mode for a sound check doesn't accurately reflect the actual sound quality, as LiveMotion uses an uncompressed version of the audio file. Always test the exported SWF file.

White Bone Demon

Red Guard Heaven: Adding Sound to Web Buttons

Attaching sound to your Web site's rollover buttons is a nice interactive touch. An audible reaction to the push of a button not only mirrors the real world, but (on the Web) also adds an element of surprise and fun. It encourages your visitors to explore your site.

LiveMotion makes applying sounds to a button object easy. I'll show you how to add sound to the buttons in my animation of a gung-ho Red Guard—you can follow along by adding buttons and sound to your own animation.

1. After creating a rollover button, decide which state you wish to attach your sound to—Over, Out, Down, or all of the above. For the simple Flash animation *Red Guard Heaven* (Figure 10-7), I used the Pop Down sound effect that comes with LiveMotion.

Figure 10-7: Attaching a sound to a button's Down state.

2. Attach the sound to the rollover button from the Rollovers palette (displayed by pressing F11) by first highlighting the Down state and then clicking the Sound icon. From the Open dialog box, navigate to LiveMotion's secret stash of sound files (Adobe • LiveMotion • Sounds) and double-click on the file PopDown.aif.

3. Test the effect in your browser.

Unlike sound objects that have been inserted or dragged into a composition, a sound effect applied to a Rollover state doesn't appear in the Timeline. Rather, it's hidden in the Rollovers palette under Changes (right below the layer you've attached it to). You'll have to click the twisty to reveal it (Figure 10-8). To delete a sound, highlight it in the palette and click the trash icon.

Figure 10-8: The hidden sound effect.

Slim It Down?

Let's look at the stats to see how much the sound adds to the file size.

I exported *Red Guard Heaven* to SWF format with the image of Mao in JPEG format. (GIF would not have reproduced the gradu-ated texture in the background.) The Quality setting was 35, opac-ity was 4, and the frame rate was 10 fps. The final .swf file was 28K.

When I exported another version of the file—this time with-out the sound but with otherwise identical settings, the final Flash was 27K. So omitting the sound effect here would not speed up the download, and the animation would be far less effective.

You can preview both versions at www.littleredbooks.com/heaven.htm.

See the difference a little AIFF can make?

Duplicating Objects with Sounds

If you want to duplicate a button with its sound effect intact, select it in the composition and choose Edit • Make Alias to place a copy of the button directly on top of the original. Then simply drag it to the desired position.

Alien Sounds: Adding a Soundtrack

Let's use a couple of extraterrestrial effects to create a soundtrack for the *Birth of an Alien* Flash animation from Chapter 8.

Getting Ready

1. Create a project folder called Alien on your desktop, and download alien.zip from www.littleredbooks.com/download/alien.zip. Extract it to your folder, and you'll find the following three files: myalien.liv, sound1.aif, and sound2.aif.

2. Copy the two .aif sound files to the LiveMotion Sounds subfolder on your hard drive (…/Program Files/Adobe/LiveMotion/Sounds).

3. Double-click myalien.liv to open the file in LiveMotion, and press CTRL-T to bring up the Timeline.

    When moving the CTM in this exercise, the counter in the upper left corner of the Timeline indicates the CTM's position; when you drag an object's duration bar, however, the counter will not change.

4. Click on the composition's title bar to make it active, then press Q to enter Preview mode and view the animation. The animation plays for just under 14 seconds.

5. Press Q again to return to Edit mode, which resets the CTM at 00.

Adding sound1

We're going to add two sounds: a weird alien wind, which we'll loop (sound1), and an eerie electronic effect (sound2) to accompany the appearance of the creature that zooms out of the alien's eye and fades away. We'll manipulate this sound so that it fades out along with the image.

1. From the Sounds palette, select sound1 and preview it by clicking the Play Sound button.

2. Click the Apply Sound button. "sound1 (Event)" now appears in the Timeline list (Figure 10-9).

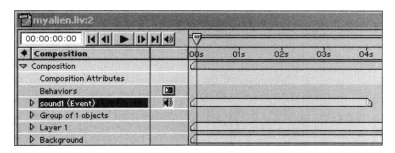

Figure 10-9: The "sound1 (Event)" object in the Timeline.

3. Click on the composition's title bar to make it active, press Q, and preview the animation. (Press Q again when it stops.)

4. Press CTRL-S to save the file.

Looping sound1 and Adding sound2

Our sound ends at 04s, about 9 seconds too soon. We'll fix that by making it a TIG and looping it.

1. Select "sound1 (Event)" in the Timeline list. From the menu, choose Timeline • Make Time Independent Group. The sound now appears as "Group of 1 Objects." Press ENTER and rename it "sound Group1." Click OK or press ENTER to close the box.

2. Double-click "sound Group1" in the list to jump to the TIG Timeline. Select "sound Group1" at the top of the list (*not* the "sound Group1" label at the very top—see Figure 10-10), and click the Loop button at the bottom of the Timeline.

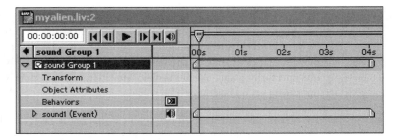

Figure 10-10: The "sound Group1" object highlighted in the Timeline.

3. Click the Play button to test it; click the Stop button when done. Click the black arrow next to the "sound Group1" label to return to the main Timeline.

4. Click Composition at the top of the Timeline list to select it. While keeping an eye on the counter, drag the CTM to 09.06. This is where the creature in the alien's eye starts to fade in.

5. In the Sounds palette, select sound2 and click the Apply Sound button. The Timeline should now resemble the one in Figure 10-11.

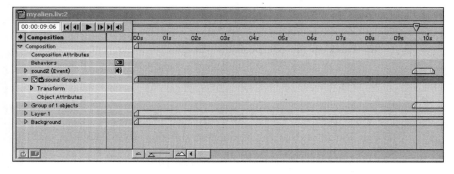

Figure 10-11: Alien Timeline with two sounds.

6. Press CTRL-S to save the file. Click on the composition's title bar to make it active, press Q to preview your work, and press Q again to stop when done.

Extending and Fading Out sound2

The soundtrack is not bad, but we want to time sound2 (Event) so that it continues while the graphic remains on screen and then fades out along with the graphic.

1. Drag the CTM to 13:05 (where the graphic fades out).

2. Click the right grabber at the end of the sound2 (Event) duration bar, and drag it to the last frame of the animation (13:08); now the sound repeats until the end of the animation. Figure 10-12 shows the extended sound effect. (The seven vertical lines in the object's duration bar represent each iteration of the sound.)

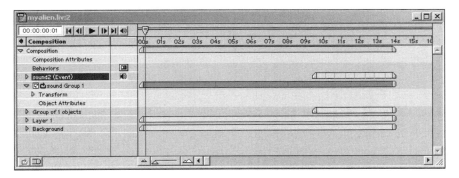

Figure 10-12: The sound2 (Event) object stretched in the Timeline.

3. Click on the composition's title bar to make it active, press Q to preview it, and press Q again to return to Edit mode.

4. Now let's make sound2 fade out. Move the CTM to sound2's first frame at 09:06.

5. Select "sound2 (Event)" in the list and click its twisties to reveal the Object Attributes.

6. Click Volume to set a keyframe at 09:06. Keep your eye on the composition and drag the CTM to 12s. We'll begin to fade the sound here.

7. In the Properties palette (displayed by pressing F8), drag the Volume slider bar to 70.

8. Drag the CTM to 12:05.

9. In the Properties palette, drag the Volume slider bar to 22 (Figure 10-13).

10. Finally, drag the CTM to 13:04 and set the Volume to 0. Press CTRL-S to save your work.

Now preview the animation in your browser and check the export report. You should find the file size to be 58.37K, with 143 frames at 10 fps.

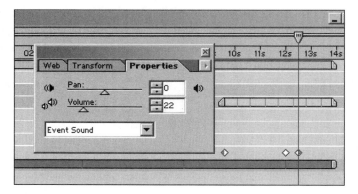

Figure 10-13: Fading the sound.

Red Guard Mission (Possible): Reduce File Size

Your assignment, should you choose to accept it, is to cut down the animation's file size before exporting it as an SWF (Flash) animation. Before you begin, read the following section on exporting sound. You can also refer to Chapter 8 for additional tips.

I managed, after tinkering with the settings, to reduce the file size to 36K. You can view it at www.littleredbooks.com/myalien.htm. Match it or do better.

Exporting Sound to Flash

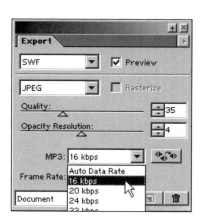

Before exporting to SWF format, you can change your sound settings to affect sound quality or decrease the overall size of your file. Simply select your sound in the Timeline, and then make any changes in the Export palette shown in Figure 10-14.

If you're just beginning to experiment with sound, the default Auto Data Rate setting is a safe bet. Sixteen kbps offers the highest compression but the lowest quality. This setting is

Figure 10-14: Setting the rate of MP3 compression.

fine for short sound effects (with buttons, for example), but would be too low for a stereo music clip for your Web site's splash screen. On the other hand, a setting of 160 kbps for an extended musical clip will increase download time considerably and probably require you to add a preloader. Ultimately—as with the quality settings for graphics—the process is one of trial and error, depending on the nature of the sound objects and how you employ them.

Each sound object in an animation can have a unique setting. Just select a sound and choose Object from the Export palette's bottom menu. The default setting, Document, applies changes to all of the sounds in the composition. The button to the right of the MP3 setting lets you convert stereo clips to mono, which can also aid in reducing the size of your final Flash file.

Load Movies! Fire Flash! Bang!

In 1989, I published a work of experimental fiction called *Assassination Rhapsody*,[6] based on the Warren Commission's report on the assassination of President John F. Kennedy. Over the years, I've often thought about producing a multimedia version of *Rhapsody*—either Web or CD based—and I even created a rough Flash intro. *The Little Red Book* has given me the opportunity to take a tiny step forward toward this potential project. I'm including it here for two reasons: (1) I think it shows that a well-timed sound effect is worth a thousand words; and (2) it makes use of the Load Movie behavior, which we haven't yet discussed.

I hope *Rhapsody* will inspire you to take a cinematic approach to sound. A "splash screen" for your Web site is a lot like a movie trailer or a film's pre-credit sequence—a great way to entice visitors to click and enter while at the same time setting a mood that serves your content. Before proceeding, view this work in progress on the Web at www.littleredbooks.com/rhapsody.htm.

Although it appears as one animation, *Rhapsody* is actually made up of two separate .swf files. The first, leadin.swf (4K), has no sound; it features the date "November 22, 1963" fading in on a black background, followed by a sniper's scope that zooms in and fades away. The second file, titles1.swf (9K), opens with the sound of a gunshot in the darkness. Then the shadowy image of a screaming face (taken from the book's cover) fades in and vanishes, as two more shots ring out. With a good sound system, the gunshots really reverberate for a chilling effect.

I had one glitch—my original .liv file with the attached sound was missing from my backup disk. (A conspiracy, no doubt.) Since LiveMotion doesn't import .swf files, I used the Load Movie behavior to join the two animations, rather than re-create the file from scratch.

---

[6] Published in the Foreign Agents Series by Semiotext(e) (New York: 1989).

The Load Movie Behavior

The Load Movie behavior tells one SWF movie to load (or append) another, allowing you to blend multiple animations seamlessly into one. It's also a handy technique for dividing a movie into "scenes." You can even use this behavior to build an entirely Flash-based Web site (see Chapter 12).

But why would you want to load movies separately? One reason is to clean up cluttered Timelines. Another is to decrease download time by breaking up a file with multiple sounds and bitmaps.

Adding Load Movie to Rhapsody

Here's how I added the Load Movie behavior to Rhapsody's first animation.

In the Timeline for leadin.liv, I dragged the CTM to a point near the end of the animation where I wanted the second Flash movie to replace it, and then I clicked the Behaviors icon (circled in Figure 10-15) to launch the Edit Behaviors dialog box.

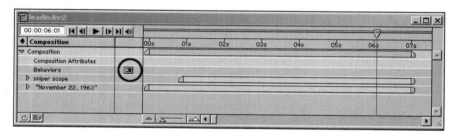

Figure 10-15: The Good Behaviors icon.

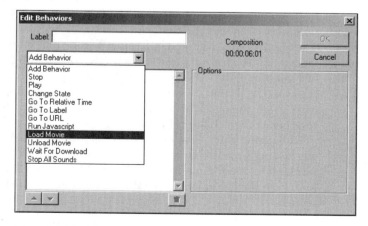

Figure 10-16: Selecting Load Movie from the Add Behaviors menu.

From the Add Behavior drop-down menu, I selected Load Movie (Figure 10-16). Although not necessary, I typed "Load Movie" in the Label entry box so you'd easily spot the behavior on the Timeline.

In the URL list box, I typed the name of the file I wanted to load (Figure 10-17). Since both movie files were in the same folder, the file name alone was sufficient. I left the default Replace option checked, as I wanted the second movie to replace the first, rather than be appended to it. (The Append option is necessary when you want two movies to run simultaneously—see Chapter 12 for an example.) Figure 10-18 shows the Timeline with the new behavior added.

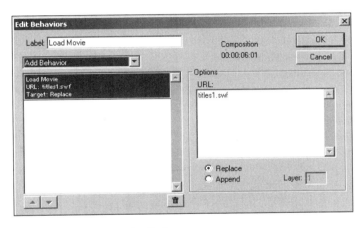

Figure 10-17: Targeting the Flash movie.

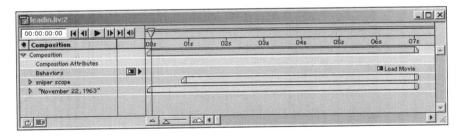

Figure 10-18: Timeline with the Load Movie behavior added.

And that's a Rhap!

You may be wondering whether the Chinese Communists had anything to do with JFK's assassination. Well, based on my examination of the evidence, all I can say is . . . sure, why not?

If a Tree Falls in the Red Forest . . .

I'll end this chapter with an instructive historical anecdote.

Mao Zedong has been widely criticized for his disastrous economic five-year plan (*Yi wu ji hua*, 1953–1957). In 1954, Premier Zhou Enlai directed a hapless foot soldier in the People's Animation Army—Yoo Fung (Figure 10-19)—to deliver the news to the Chairman that his policy was a flop. Surely, no one in the leadership of the CCP dared inform Mao that he'd goofed on so grand a scale.

Trembling in his boots, Yoo Fung entered the Chairman's private chambers at Zhongnanhai and stood before the Great Helmsman himself.

Fung was Tse-tung-tied.

"Speak up!" barked Mao. "I don't have all day."

The nervous soldier—certain that his fate would be execution—proceeded to read from a long document describing the failures of the "Five-Year Plan." When the messenger finally finished reading the report, Mao stared at him for a long moment before remarking, *"Wha?"*

Figure 10-19: Yoo Fung, messenger boy and martyr.

Yoo Fung was executed that very afternoon—charged with the obscure crime of *mumbling against the State.*

It seems years of sitting in the front row at Red Guard rock concerts had taken its toll on the Chairman's ears.

Had Mao been able to hear the voice of Yoo Fung, history might well have been different.

So you see, sound (or lack of it) can make all the difference in the world.

Uncle Mao's Instant Preloader.

11

CAPITALIST FREELOADERS AND PROLETARIAN PRELOADERS

1. Make tiny animation TIG and loop it (00s to 01s).
2. Set fat main animation to start after 01s.
3. Add "Start" label at 00s.
4. Add "End" label at last frame in fat main animation.
5. Add "Wait for Download" behavior at 01s, with a Loop setting of Start, an Until setting of End. Serve HOT!

To keep those fidgety Red Guards from surfing away from your slow-loading Flash animation, you can use a preloader—an entertaining mini-movie that loops in advance of the main attraction.

To me, the word preloader has a whiff of the pejorative. It sounds vapid, functional, and dull. Maybe that's why so many Web designers are uninspired when it comes to making one. Visit a dozen Flash-based sites and you'll see what I mean. No pun intended, but nine times out of ten you'll find either a countdown, a download bar gauge, or those monotonous flickering running dogs . . . loading . . . loading . . . loading . . . .

Freeloader preloaders, that's what I call them.

A deftly timed knock-knock joke would be preferable. Bring me the head of Porky Pig and have it zoom in and out. Give me

Chairman Mao spinning in his grave. Even a line of text that types itself out: "You know, a funny thing happened on the way to the animation. . . ."

It's a cruel fact, but Web surfers are a restless breed. They won't throw vegetables and make faces at the monitor; they'll simply click and leave. That's why your preloader should distract them. It can be as flamboyant as a carnival barker or as subtle as "Pssst—take a look at this." whispered from the shadows. Whatever it is, it must hold their attention until the big file loads. The challenge is to make the preloader interesting without making it heavy in and of itself.

One of the best preloaders I've ever seen was on Shockwave. com. Visitors were given the option of playing a shooting gallery game while waiting for the movie. The game—a vector-based cartoon—loaded quickly, complete with sound effects. It was great!

Find a Hook and Grab the Masses!

Approach the preloader with a sense of humor and you'll buy yourself some valuable download time. After all, the idea is to hook the masses and keep them from clicking the ubiquitous Skip Animation link. Be creative: Make this byte-sized teaser a visual gem and you'll have no need for an exit strategy.

That, at least, should be the goal.

Little Red Book with Hook.[1]

---

[1] Book-object by Norman Conquest.

How a Preloader Works

In a nutshell, the process of adding a preloader to an animation (or vice versa) requires inserting three behaviors: Start (at the Timeline's first frame), End (at the main animation's last frame), and Wait for Download (at the preloader's last frame). The looping preloader is positioned in the first few frames of the Timeline, and the main animation appears in the frame adjacent to the preloader.

Each time the preloader hits its final frame (Wait for Download), it checks to see whether all of the overweight elements in the main animation are ready for prime time. If not, it jumps back to the first frame and continues looping.

Sure, it's a thankless task, but such is the fate of the downtrodden preloader.

Waiting for Download: Implementing a Preloader

The preloader screen shot shown in Figure 11-1 is part of a visual pun consisting of two frustrated figures running back and forth. Surely, if Beckett was alive today, he'd write a novel about two nerds trapped as preloaders in purgatory, awaiting the ultimate Flash from heaven.

Figure 11-1: Preloader à la Samuel Beckett.

For the two figures, I used Leslie Wagren's delightful dingbat font, DanceMan. The title was set in the Stereo Hifi typeface, which matches the style of the figures nicely. Not a bitmap in sight, mind you. These three objects are all type elements—tiny byte-sized vectors. After animating the position of the figures, I had a file weighing only 2.38K. For someone using an ancient 14.4 kbps modem, the animation will load in under 2 seconds, and with a 56 kbps modem it loads in the blink of an eye.

Make someone wait for your preloader to load and you'd better buy a bullet-proof vest.

Bear in mind that—to paraphrase Neil Simon—it's a lot easier for you to see the preloader that I'm explaining than it is for me to explain the preloader that you're seeing. Perhaps that's why most of the current crop of books on LiveMotion (including Adobe's own *LiveMotion User Guide*) don't even mention preloaders.

But being the brave little red soldiers that we are, we'll press forward, and together we'll implement this cute little preloader by placing it in front of a fat bourgeois capitalist animation.

Preloader Preparations

Before we add the preloader, we must first have something to add it to. Let's prepare the preloader files and the main animation.

1. Download the font (danceman.zip) from www.littleredbooks. com/download/danceman.zip and the preloader (godot.zip) from www.littleredbooks.com/download/godot.zip to a project folder on your desktop. Unzip godot.zip.

2. Unzip danceman.zip and copy the TrueType file into your Fonts folder to install it on your system (Start • Settings • Control Panel • Fonts). If you're using a Mac, just drop the font onto your System folder.

3. Launch LiveMotion and create a new composition sized 500 x 500.

4. Set the background color to black.

5. Drag the composition's duration bar to 10s—that'll give you plenty of time for an eye-grabbing Flash.

6. Before placing or creating your objects, set the CTM to one frame past 01s (the CTM should be aligned with the small *s*), as you want to leave room on the Timeline for the preloader.

7. Now make a fat capitalist of an animation to which you'll add the preloader. Feel free to be extravagant. Use a few big bitmaps and assorted objects with fancy styles applied. Shoot for a file size of at least 50K. Preview your animation in the browser and run an export report to check the size. If the file is too small, go to the Export palette and increase the quality setting. I used a bulky 80K animation depicting Mao's reaction to this book. (See the section "The Main Attraction" later in this chapter.)

Adding the Preloader

Now we'll add the preloader to the main animation. Figure 11-2 shows the preloader Timeline and its three component objects: the title, right tramp, and left tramp.

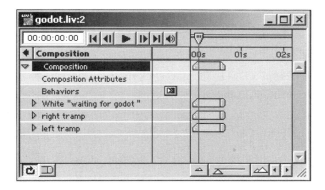

Figure 11-2: Preloader Timeline.

1. Set your main animation to begin at one frame past 01s in the Timeline. Move the CTM to 00s.

2. Open godot.liv. For the sake of simplicity, I've removed the title text "waiting for godot." Resize the windows if necessary so you can access both the preloader and main animations.

3. Press CTRL-A to select the stick figures in the preloader, and press CTRL-C to copy them to the Clipboard.

4. Close the preloader file, and click on the title bar of your animation to make it active. Make sure the CTM is set at 00s.

5. Press CTRL-V to paste the preloader into the first frame of the composition.

6. From the Timeline menu, choose Time Independent Group.

7. Center the figures by clicking their bounding boxes with the selection tool and dragging them to center of the composition.

8. Press CTRL-T to bring up the Timeline. "Group of 2 Objects" will appear highlighted in the list. Press ENTER and type "Preloader." Click OK. The preloader is now in place.

NOTE *If the preloader's duration bar extends to the end of the main animation, drag it back and make it end at 01s. Otherwise, the figures will become anarchists, running rampant through the entire animation.*

Let's take stock of where we are (to make sure there are no rightist-leftist freaks among us, of course). Our animation consists of two sections: an animation that runs during the first portion of the Timeline and the main animation that follows. We now want to apply the appropriate labels and behaviors to tell LiveMotion about the Great Wall that exists between these two sections.

Setting the Gang of Three Behaviors

As of the moment, our preloader is like a nested spy awaiting orders from his handler. Let's get the subversion rolling.

1. Set the CTM to 00s and click the Behaviors icon.

2. In the Edit Behaviors box, type "Start" in the Label box. Click OK.

3. Drag the CTM to the last frame of your main animation and click the Behaviors icon.

4. In the Edit Behaviors box, type "End" for the Label. Click OK.

5. Drag the CTM to 01s and click the Behaviors icon.

6. In the Edit Behaviors box, click the Add Behavior arrow and select Wait for Download from the list.

7. Set the Loop option to Start and the Until option to End. Click OK.

8. In the Timeline list, double-click on Preloader to open its independent Timeline (Figure 11-3). Click on Preloader at the top of the list to highlight it, then click the loop arrow in the bottom left corner of the Timeline.

The nested preloader now has its orders and is ready to loop in service of the great and bloated Mao Zedong.

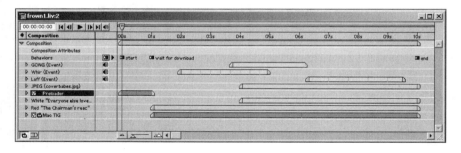

Figure 11-3: Timeline showing preloader and the Gang of Three behaviors.

The Main Attraction

My main attraction (Figure 11-4) is appropriately hefty, as it features the following objects: an animated bitmap of Mao's face (a looping TIG), a bitmap image of an early version of this book's cover, animated text, and three sound files (a whir, a gong, and a laugh). These components made for an .swf file of 83K, which definitely required the preloader.

Figure 11-4: Bloated Mao, bloated animation.

You'll want to preview your animation before exporting it as a Flash file. Remember, however, that viewing the file on your hard drive will *not* accurately portray the preloader's behavior, since the main animation will load quickly. The only way to really test the work is to upload it to the Web and then view it in your browser.

To view the *Godot* preloader in action, go to www.littleredbooks.com/rave.htm.

White Bone
Demon

If you preview the animation inside LiveMotion, you'll see that, due to the Wait for Download behavior, the CTM will keep jumping back to the designated point. LiveMotion doesn't know how quickly your Net connection will download the composition, so it will keep looping until the world is united in socialist brotherhood (that is, indefinitely). To tell LiveMotion that the download is complete, hold down CTRL while previewing.

Rebel with a Cause

I don't want to leave you with the impression that it's OK to make giant-sized Flash animations for the hell of it just because you can always pop in a preloader. No matter how good a preloader is, it's still a *preloader*. Unless you cleverly disguise it to appear as the main

Rebel inside.

animation, viewers will know that they're essentially standing in line with their tickets, waiting for the show to start.

On the other hand, if you need a deeply interactive animation requiring bitmaps and sound, your animation could easily exceed 100K. In such cases a preloader must be deployed.

The Little Preloader That Could

Often the butt of jokes, the preloader is like the five-year-old boy who dons his big brother's Red Guard armband and, Little Red Book in hand, marches back and forth, proclaiming the glories of Mao Zedong Thought, his head full of visions of one day being a full-fledged soldier in the People's Army—bravely defending the Republic from imperialist invaders and fire-breathing CEOs.

A carefully crafted little preloader may, indeed, contain the seeds of a full-fledged animation. Perhaps it too will realize its dreams and someday require a preloader of its own.

Early portrait of the Great Helmsman.

12

THE CULT OF MOTION:
Building Great
Socialist Web Sites

In the immortal words of Chairman Mao,
Build it, and they will buy.

He was, of course, referring to the Great Hall of
Memorabilia, where souvenirs plastered with his vis-
age are sold to tourists all year long: Mao teacups, cigarette lighters, cookie jars, toothbrushes, money clips,
and little red handbags.

Seeing Mao as the visionary that he was, the People's Animation
Army interprets this quote as a radical pronouncement paving the
path to e-communism. But this raises a perplexing conundrum:
Why, if they were clearly following the ideologically correct line with
great zeal, did the Dot-Commies drop like flies?

Maybe their banner ads lacked the subtle elegance of the one
depicted in Figure 12-1. Or perhaps they were suffering a Brand
Identity Crisis and had lost their ideological souls by ignoring the
tenets of Mao Zedong Thought and the Three Principles of Web-
Building:

1. **Infiltrate.** Plant seeds of revolt in cyberspace, let a thousand
   dot-COMs (Cults of Motion) bloom.

2. **Animate.** Deploy Adobe LiveMotion to spread animated Flash
   propaganda far and wide.

3. **Dominate the Web**. Seize the Internet by farce and declare
   victory.

Figure 12-1. Great and glorious banner ad.

The Web Is in Its Infancy (And It's a Brat)

The Web is the Cultural Revolution run amok. Or, if clichés are your cup of tea, it's the Wild West. Anarchic, turbulent, a vast sea of spam, spies, hoaxes, viruses, porn cults, hacker claques, glittering litter, Drudge, and DoS.[1] It's a cosmic supermarket tabloid gone berserk.

And just try to make yourself heard on the Net, Comrades. It is no easy task; it's like shouting "Fire!" at a Red Guard rally. You will be drowned out by the din. Then again, the Web is *awesome.* And it really is possible to make a ripple on the surface, if not a giant splash. But whether your splash be little or big, LiveMotion can help. It will work with you at every stage, from fermenting navigation schemes and testing layouts to adding splash screens and Flashing your content so it rises like a shining Red Star.

As I write these words, www.littleredbooks.com is still in the concept stage, "e-volving" slowly and subject to change without notice. In other words, it's an ideal test site for this chapter. We'll explore a few sample Flash layouts, use some advanced behaviors and a snippet of code, and prepare for the great leap into the Net.

Serving the Revolution: Plan Your Web Site Well

There are as many approaches to planning a Web site as there are Mao buttons. I won't attempt to explore the nature of site architecture, nor the science and philosophy of design. I'll leave that to talented gurus like Roger Black, Jeffrey Veen, and Lynda Weinman.[2] This chapter assumes that you have your goals in mind and that you know your content and target audience. Beyond that, it's smoke, mirrors, and books on Web site usability filled with graphs that "illuminate" market research tests with real-world lab data. If you dig deeper, you can find studies on the psychology of why Lab Rat 42 pushes Web Button A rather than B and which Web-safe color scheme encourages visitors to click the shopping cart icon.

---

[1] Denial of Service attack, not to be confused with DOS, that Enemy of the People created by Chairman Bill.
[2] See Appendix B for some resources containing practical and theoretical approaches to Web architecture.

Communist sympathizers from the U.S.A. help serve the un-revolution.

I say *bull.* You can analyze the nature of greed until the Maos come home, but that won't make your site a creative success. So what will? Try the Motion Patrol's approach: *Make it fun, and have fun making it.*

Fit your style to your content. For example, is it "bad design" to have www.littleredbooks.com resemble a Chinese take-out menu? Or is it "good design" because it fits the content perfectly?

As a LiveMotioneer, learn to discard all running-dog labels. Break the rules and serve the Revolution. "To rebel is good!" said Mao. Let us heed the Chairman and make our designs serve our propaganda.

Little Red Layout Dreams

LiveMotion was made for plotting layouts that thoroughly smash the old ways. Manipulate your objects at will, torture them, purge them as you please. Design a dozen Mao buttons and change them all with a click of the mouse. Undo rightist errors and bravely forge ahead. When at last you have your revolutionary design just the way you want it, you can export it directly to HTML or SWF format.

You'll save yourself a lot of time if you arrive at the computer armed with a concept. As I mentioned, I keep a little red notebook for sketching layouts and jotting down commie visions. When uninspired, I just dip into my bowl of Chinese doodles, pluck one out, and test it in LiveMotion. Does it have snap, crackle, and pop—like Maoist fireworks—or does it fizzle out like a reactionary dud?

People's Layout #1

Let's take a look at some designs that show promise.

LiveMotion lets you work with multiple files simultaneously—indispensable for plotting Web layouts. In Figure 12-2, I have two home page designs for Little Red Books open side by side.

Figure 12-2: Comparing layouts and trying on styles.

After making the top navigation rollover button, I pressed CTRL-M four times and generated four copies—each an alias. That way, I could apply different styles and shapes to the original and—with one click of the mouse—cause the others to follow suit like an obedient cadre in service to Mao. On the left I tried a rounded rectangle shape for the buttons; on the right I used an ellipse. Were the buttons too big?[3] No problem—scaling down one button will scale its aliases down as well.

I swapped background colors, tested different fonts for the button text, and purged and rehabilitated a dozen portraits of the

---

[3] As a Web Guard designer, you should engage in fervent self-criticism. Attack yourself for plotting faulty navigation schemes: "Forgive my wicked, hegemonist ways. I made all my links the same color as my background. Beat my head with bamboo sticks!" It's always easier to create a great-looking site than it is to make it People-Friendly.

Chairman in search of the "correct" combination. Since LiveMotion makes it easy to transform every element, the problem quickly becomes, *Which one should I choose?*

My design evolved to the variation shown in Figure 12-3. It has what is technically know as *ZIP.*[4] It's your basic proletarian design—bold and functional, with its message animated for extra emphasis. No filler, no fluff, no artificial ingredients.

Figure 12-3: The People's Layout #1 in LiveMotion.

Remaining aware of ultimate file size, I kept the number of objects in the composition to a minimum: A simple black rectangle behind the buttons, a vector[5] image of Mao (rotated for added smugness), and two small black rectangles above and below the image to underscore the masthead's flaglike appearance and anchor the design. To echo the flag motif, I imported an animated GIF of the PRC flag and made it a TIG. (Sorry for all the acronyms but I'm an acronymphomaniac.)

Finally, I swiped a vector starburst shape from the Library palette and positioned it behind the word *rebel.* I then grouped the two objects and animated the group's opacity and scale to produce a zoom effect.

The only bitmaps in this layout are the rollover buttons, and their size was minimal, so the final exported .swf file came in at a respectable 18K. (See Chapter 8 for more information on exporting to SWF format.)

You can view the layout at www.littleredbooks.com/layout1.htm. The links, however, are not active.

---

[4] Zedongian Internet Principle #1: "Be bold and functional!"
[5] The original graphic was a bloated bourgeois bitmap, which I "reeducated" to vectorhood via CorelTRACE.

HTML and bitmap images can't preserve all the socialist flavor of Flash, including Flash's ability to have buttons and animated objects passing over one another. When designing a layout for autosliced HTML (for more information on sliced HTML, see Chapter 8), be sure to keep rollovers and animations from overlapping, lest you encounter a dreaded error message.

White Bone
Demon

Exporting to HTML

When you're not exporting as a Flash animation, the AutoSlice feature lets you save your design and JavaScript rollovers as HTML —in fraternal socialist fashion; that is, WYSIWYG. For our example layout, if I wanted to keep a static version of the *rebel* type and the starburst, I'd purge the zooming effect from the Timeline (by turning off the opacity and scale stopwatches) and export via AutoSlice. To use the flag animation in HTML, I'd open the exported HTML page in my editing program, Dreamweaver, and insert it into the table generated by LiveMotion.

Exporting to Frames

To export the People's Layout from LiveMotion into a frame based Web site (so that the navigation buttons remain visible at all times while loading linked pages in another frame), export with the AutoSlice option, but in addition to adding a Go to URL behavior to each rollover button separately (by selecting the but-

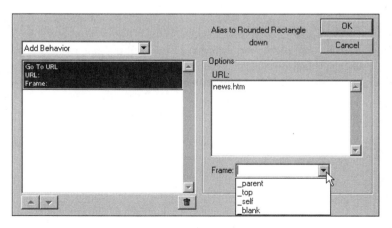

Figure 12-4: Targeting a frame in the Edit Behaviors dialog box.

ton's Down state in the Rollovers palette and clicking the Behaviors button), also set the target frame for each from the Frame drop-down menu (Figure 12-4). After exporting, open the HTML file that LiveMotion generates, and copy and paste the appropriate sections to the HTML pages that make up the frame set.

Flash-Based "Manchurian Candidate" Layout: Using the Load Movie Behavior

Let's look at a Web layout that uses the Load Movie behavior.

Figure 12-5 shows a Flash home page *(The Mainland)* that uses the Load Movie behavior. I attempted to catch the audience off their Red Guard by opening with what appears to be an apple on a hillock. Suddenly the hillock rises up (Figure 12-6), a gong crashes (an AIF sound effect), and it turns out to be my drawing of Mao. The vector explosion shape (a looping TIG) shifts back and forth behind the Chairman's head.

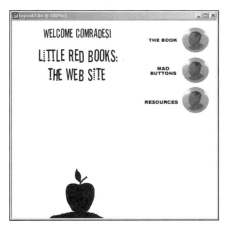

Figure 12-5: Flash layout.

Figure 12-6: Mao on the rise.

By placing three rollover buttons in the upper right, I departed from Leftist tradition in order to balance the composition. The buttons face the logo and emphasize the *Little Red Book's* brand identity—hopefully searing it into the viewer's unconsciousness. To be on the safe side, I embedded my Manchurian Candidate Motion Trigger code (patent pending)—a subliminal brainwashing technique that guarantees repeat visits. Every time a viewer hears a gong, she or he will immediately seek out the nearest browser and go directly to the site. (You will now forget what

I just told you and go immediately to the following URL: www. littleredbooks.com/layout2.htm.)

If you clicked the Mao navigation buttons, you might have thought you were surfing to another page, but in reality you never left. Instead, a new Flash movie replaced the original via the Load Movie behavior. Replacing one Flash movie with another has the advantage of keeping the download size down, rather than incorporating all the elements in one big animation. Instead of waiting for all of the content to come in at once, your visitor receives the requested pieces as they stream in. (See the section "Replacing SWF Movies" later in this chapter.)

Appending a Movie to a Movie

We've seen how cool replacing one movie with another is, but if we simply *add* a movie it will wipe out the objects from the first movie. What if we want our original objects to remain on screen when the new movie loads? The answer is simple, Comrades: We turn to the Append aspect of the Load Movie behavior.

NOTE *LiveMotion appends the .swf file in the upper left corner of the composition, so make sure both files have the same dimensions.*

The following example describes how to create two simple Flash movies. The first is a heart-shaped rollover button that, when clicked, triggers another movie, which gets appended above it— three purple hearts, throbbing with devotion to the Great Helmsman.

Create the First Composition

First create the heart button.

1. Start a new composition with the following settings: 300 x 300, Frame Rate 12, AutoLayout, and Make HTML checked. Press SHIFT-CTRL-S, name the file "heart1," and save it to a project folder.

2. Fill the background with black.

3. Set the fill color to red and, in the Library palette, locate Heart and click the Place Object button to insert it in the center of the composition.

4. In the Transform palette, change the object's width and height to 104 and 112, respectively, and press ENTER. Change the Y coordinate to 177 and press ENTER again.

5. In the 3D palette, choose Emboss and set the Depth slider to a setting of your choice. (I used a Depth of 16, a Softness of 5, and the default Lighting.)

6. Click inside the composition to deselect the heart. Change the fill color to white, and add some text to place on our heart button. Make sure the text fits within the heart's outline.

7. Using the Selection tool, drag a marquee around both objects to select them. Choose Object • Combine • Unite with Color to bond the shapes in fervent socialist union.

Make the Heart into a Rollover Button and Export to SWF Format

1. Press F11 to display the Rollovers palette, and click the New Rollover State button to set the Over state.

2. In the Adjust palette, select Invert to flip the colors for the rollover effect.

3. Return to the Rollovers palette, and click the Duplicate Rollover State button to set a Down state. Click the Edit Behaviors button, and choose Load Movie from the Add Behavior menu. In the URL box, type heart2.swf and select Append. (You will create heart2.swf next.) Click OK, and press CTRL-S to save your work.

4. Choose File • Export, accept the default name, heart1.swf, and click Save. (The file should be stored in your project folder. LiveMotion automatically creates an HTML file along with the .swf files.) Close the file.

Create the Movie to Append

1. Start a new composition with the same settings as for the heart rollover: 300 x 300, Frame Rate 12, AutoLayout, and Make HTML checked. Press SHIFT-CTRL-S, name the file "heart2," and save it to a project folder.

2. Fill the background with black.

3. Change the fill color to purple and place another Heart object from the Library.

4. In the Transform palette, resize the object's width and height to 39 and 42, respectively. Press ENTER.

5. Drag the heart to the upper left of the composition. Launch the Timeline (CTRL -T), and press ENTER. Name the object Purple Heart and click OK.

6. Set the composition duration bar to 00:06. With the CTM set at 00, click the twisties for Purple Heart to reveal the

Transform attributes. Click the stopwatch next to Scale to insert a keyframe (diamond) in the Timeline.

7. Move the CTM to the first frame. In the Transform palette, resize the heart's width and height to 64 and 70, respectively, and press ENTER.

8. Click Purple Heart in the Timeline list. Drag the CTM to the third frame (00:03). Then, holding down the ALT key, position your cursor over the first diamond. When the cursor becomes a double arrow, click and drag the diamond to the third frame. (By holding down the ALT key, you create a copy of the first keyframe, saving a few steps.)

9. Click to select Composition in the Timeline list, and click the loop button at the lower left. (If you want to preview your work at this stage, choose File • Preview In and check it in the browser. At this stage, Preview mode will not be accurate because you're loading an external .swf file.)

Add Two More Throbbing Hearts

1. Select the heart in the composition and press CTRL-M twice to place two aliases directly on top of the original. Drag each copy off to the right. Arrange the hearts in the approximate position shown in Figure 12-7.

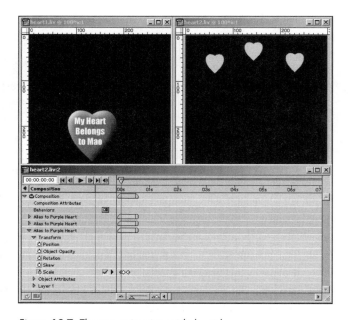

Figure 12-7: The two animations side by side.

2. Press CTRL-S to save the .liv file.

3. Choose File • Export, and name the .swf file "heart2."

White Bone
Demon

To create an alias by dragging, hold down ALT and SHIFT before dragging an object. If you just want to make a copy but move it in a straight line relative to the original, ALT-drag the object and start pressing SHIFT *after* you've begun dragging.

You're done!

Now open your project folder and double-click heart1.html to preview the animation in your browser. Click the button to launch the appended movie. (LiveMotion's Preview In command can't be used to test Load Movie behaviors. You have to launch the HTML file directly and preview the movie in a browser.)

NOTE *Loaded movies align their upper left corners and inherit the base .swf file's frame rate.*

Replacing SWF Movies

If you need to, you can replace one loaded movie with another by loading it into the same level. This technique lets you, for example, create an interface in which a row of buttons at the bottom calls up different chunks of content. You'll find it very useful if, say, you have ten technical (or Socialist) illustrations and you want your visitors to be able to browse to whichever they want without needing to have the others stream in.

Opening Movies in Multiple Windows

You may be asking yourselves, "Why load a movie in a separate window?"

Good question, Comrades!

Opening movies in new windows is definitely not for laissez-faire Leftists, but it's a cool way to keep the main navigation page[6] handy while the visitor surfs your site. It can also enliven a static layout and provide unique ways to present your content. Using

---

[6] An alternative to HTML frames.

multiple windows, you could, for example, divide a large graphic into animated segments.

Cartoonists could make their characters communicate from separate "apartment" windows.

Imagine the possibilities for experimental writing and hyper-text fiction!

And don't forget sound. Imagine a Gang of Four Windows—each with its own music track that, together, form a quartet!

Entering the Red Goddess's Lair

Let's take a look at an example that uses multiple windows. The Flash-based design for the Red Goddess (www.littleredbooks.com/club1.htm) incorporates six separate movies and a technique for loading movies in separate windows.

To create an intriguing entrance that leads to the four icons that trigger my windows, I began by converting a layered Photoshop file (the Red Goddess entrance and a head shot of Mao) into LiveMotion objects (see Chapter 8). All three initial Flash animations have a Load Movie behavior in their last frame. In the opener (Figure 12-8), the Great Helmsman fades in

Figure 12-8: Entrance to the Red Goddess.

beneath the dreamlike archway. Clicking on Mao causes the two images to fade away and triggers a guitar riff that segues into the second movie (Figure 12-9), where a small neon version of the logo zooms in and out and the text glides in and fades. This brief clip serves as a bridge to the third movie, in which four animated rollover buttons fly into position above their labels (Figure 12-10).

Figure 12-9: The second movie.

Figure 12-10: The third movie.

Each button has a "click" sound and the Load Movie behavior attached to its Down state. Instead of using the Replace function when a button is clicked (as I did in Chapter 10), I have the linked movie launch in a separate window (Figure 12-11), via a snippet of JavaScript code.

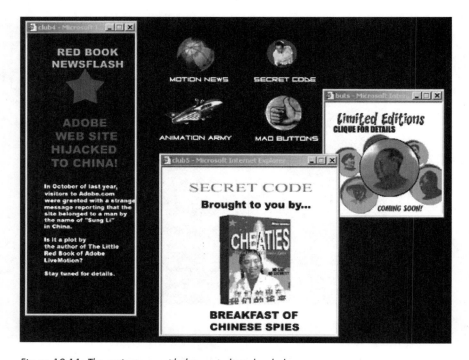

Figure 12-11: The main page with three windows loaded.

White Bone Demon

Beware of Browser Inconsistencies. Although this code will work with all browsers that support JavaScript, many scripts depend on a particular browser's (or platform's) capabilities. You should test your pages accordingly. You can create alternate versions of a page and then add a browser sniffer—JavaScript code that recognizes which browser the user has and redirects the browser automatically to the proper alternate page. But—*another demon*—sniffers don't always work as advertised. Remember, as Mao warned you, a revolution ain't no dinner party.

Loading a Movie in a New Window

Hey, I didn't mean to scare you back there by using the word *code*. I'm not now, nor have I ever been, a code junkie. But if you have the time and inclination, JavaScript[7] isn't rocket science and will enable you to extend LiveMotion's capabilities in radical ways.

So what's the Bottom Party Line?

You don't need to write your own HTML or JavaScript to build snazzy Maoist Web sites. And you don't need to *know* JavaScript to *use* JavaScript. That's right: As a member of the People's Animation Army, you can "appropriate" snippets of code and kick LiveMotion up a notch or two. After all, the ends justify the means.

Here's the secret code I used in my example (it's all one line—no hard returns):

```
var myWin=window.open("news.htm","news","scrollbars=no,width=183,height=500");
```

Is that all there is?

Yes indeed. Shorter than the Chairman's temper, this single line of JavaScript opens an HTML file (news.htm) containing a Flash movie in its own window. Just name the file and specify the size in pixels—in this case the same dimensions as the .swf file.

If you were loading an HTML page instead of a lone movie, you'd probably add a scrollbar to the window so users could get to the bottom of things. In that case, you'd simply replace "scrollbars=no" with "scrollbars=yes."

Not even close to rocket science.

See JavaScript Run

To put the code into action, I copied it to the Clipboard and, back in LiveMotion, selected the Motion News button and added the Run JavaScript command behavior (in the Add Behaviors menu) to its Down state. I then pasted the code into the JavaScript box under Options (Figure 12-12).

I followed the same procedure for the other buttons, changing the file name in the JavaScript snippet. Since all of the files were stored in the same folder, I used only the relative URL. To target a remote HTML page requires the full URL address (http:// . . .).

NOTE *You cannot use LiveMotion's Preview In command to test the JavaScript. Instead, export the file to HTML and view it in your browser.*

---

[7] A good place to start is *The Book of JavaScript* by Thau (No Starch Press).

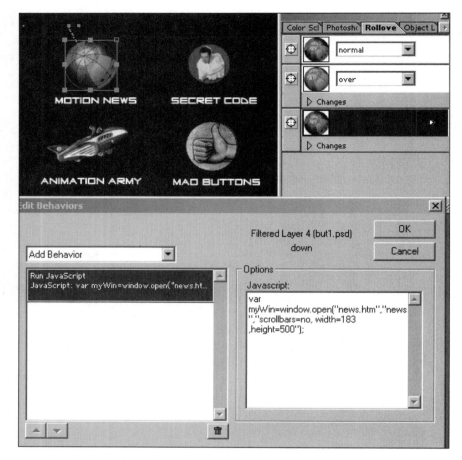

Figure 12-12: Adding the JavaScript to the button's Down state.

Theater of the Absurd

The Web can be a great space for theaters of all sorts, and
LiveMotion can help you create the layout for your theater space.
To see what I mean, surf on over to the People's Playhouse in
Beijing (www.littleredbooks.com/life.htm) and catch the show.
Don't worry; it's free. Just don't get caught talking during the
performance.

This Flash example has a funky, cartoonlike stage (Figure
12-13) that I slapped together with LiveMotion vector shapes. The
audience is not really an audience at all—it's a *font*.[8] The anima-

---

[8] StudioAudience Normal, from SnatchSoft, Inc. (See Appendix B for some
great font resources.)

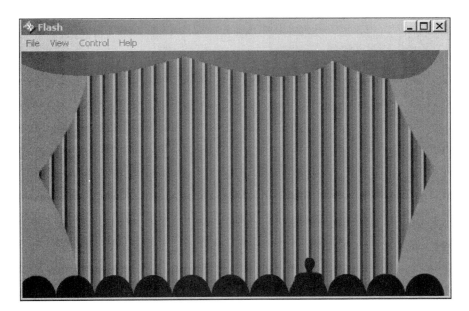

Figure 12-13: A slow night at the People's Playhouse.

tion includes several sound effects that I edited with Sound Forge 4.5, a great digital audio editing program for Windows. The whole thing loads in about 20 seconds with a 56K modem and features the Godot preloader from Chapter 11.

Not surprisingly, the People's Playhouse doesn't offer its audience a choice, but your Web theater could. In fact, you could make an entire Flash-based site using Load Movie behaviors to create a single entertainment module that lets the viewer choose which show to watch. The People's Playhouse is just a modest example of a theatrical Web space—just think of the possibilities: vaudeville, striptease, drive-in movie, TV screen, or futuristic console. There are plenty of options to explore.

Smoking (Guns) Permitted: Make Your Own Zines

There's nothing like the freedom of the electronic press. You haven't lived until you've experienced the thrill of publishing your own commuzine. You can be as radical as you want. For example, in my Flash-based publication (a snap with LiveMotion; see Figure 12-14), I advocate a radical ideology: *smoking*. You can't get more radical than that! If you're ready to light up, blow on over to www.littleredbooks.com/zine.htm. (Heads up! The buttons are just for show, they have no links.)

Figure 12-14: A Flash-based commuzine.

The .swf file for *Red Goddess: The Zine* weighs in at a respectable 17K. All of the objects here are vectors, with the exception of the bitmap pack of cigarettes. Instead of using LiveMotion's bitmapped drop-shadow style, I duplicated the logo and text (CTRL-D) and placed black-filled copies behind the originals.

The entire composition is an .swf file, with two animated elements: the pack of RG Lights that spins and drifts down into position and the Write Us link that fades in and takes its place (beside that sexy *Red Guardess* figure). The rollover buttons have a basic color-change effect—nothing fancy. It's a good example of Motion Control, as sometimes just a few touches of movement will keep the viewer interested without overpowering the content.

Make a Big Splash Screen (But Keep It Small)

LiveMotion's layout capabilities can be of immense help in creating your Flash splash screens. You can work on the splash in one window with the main page open in another, to design an effective transition between the two. For example, you can animate a vector version of your logo, having it zoom and glide across the screen and then freeze in position. When the splash dissolves, a styled bitmap version of the logo could appear in its place on the home page. You see this technique (called a *match cut*) used in films all the time.

A splash screen is like a department store window, and dressing it can be a lot of fun. For visitors who don't have the Flash plug-in, you can provide a link to Macromedia's site so they can download it and an alternate link to

your main page, in case they're too lazy. A splash screen is a way of keeping all your Red Guard razzle-dazzle up front while not interfering with the site's content. Businesses that require a no-nonsense, button-down design—a CPA, for example—can, with a splash screen, let their hair down for a few seconds, saying, "See, our content may be dull, but *we're* not."

That's the conservative approach. A more radical route is to have your splash lead to an entirely Flash-based site, effectively barring entrance to those without the plug-in.

My Webzine *Dingbat: The Monthly Review of Cool Tools* (www.dingbatmag.com) plays it middle-of-the-road. I change the splash screen every issue and sprinkle Flash items throughout the site—usually in the form of animated text headings. Folks without the plug-in can still access the vast majority of the content.

Ultimately, a splash screen is icing on the content, so it's wise to keep the bytes down and avoid having to use a preloader. The easiest way to do that is to *kill all bitmaps* with extreme prejudice. Remember, when you're uncertain of an object's status, just select it and turn on LiveMotion's Active Export Preview from the View menu. A glance at the status bar will let you know whether to purge or preserve.

Animating only text and vector shapes (stripped of all styles) can produce effective, quick-loading splash screens that will have the masses on their feet and cheering.

That said . . . I *love* bitmaps. And sometimes there's no getting around them, such as when you want a photosurrealist effect. This was the case with my lively *Red Guard Pep Rally* splash in Figure 12-15.

I tried tracing the bitmap, but it just didn't deliver the look I was after. With a vector I could have gone "full-screen" with the image, but here I had to kept the image small.

Figure 12-15: Red Guard Pep Rally.

Before exporting to SWF format, I inserted a Go to URL behavior in the last frame of the animation to send the viewer to the Little Red Books main page automatically.

Opening the HTML page in Dreamweaver, I added a hyperlink for hyper-impatient communards. Then I realized something was missing. Although I was pleased with the animation, the page itself lacked a sense of depth. So I placed a tiled image of the Chairman in the background (Figure 12-16), and that did the trick. When viewed on the Web, the animation gives you the feeling of being in a huge stadium, as the Red Guard cheerleaders perform for a thousand Maos.

If you find your ideological fervor starting to fade, attend my Red Guard Pep Rally at www.littleredbooks.com/rally.htm. I guarantee you'll feel rejuvenated.

Nixon's Missing Gift to Chairman Mao

Although much has been written about President Richard M. Nixon's historic visit to China in February 1972, a few significant details remained unknown—that is, until recently. On January 12, 2001, the Beijing government unlocked the doors of Mao's personal storage vault located in a well-guarded compound in Zhongnanhai.

Figure 12-16: The finished 10K Flash splash.

A list of more than 2,000 items stored there was published in a 20-page supplement to the *People's Daily* under the headline "The World's Gifts to Chairman Mao Zedong." The list included offerings from visiting heads of state. For example, there were 10 cases of aged brandy from Romania's Ceausescu, 50 carved wooden boxes of Cuban cigars from Castro, priceless jewels from the shah of Iran, and a Fabergé egg sent by Stalin.

I read through the entire list and was struck by one glaring omission: There was no gift attributed to Richard Nixon. *Why?*

It was inconceivable that the president of the United States could have made a gaffe of such magnitude. Certainly not with the advance planning that went into that particular trip.

Could the gift have been stolen from the compound? That seemed even more unlikely. Why hadn't the thief also taken the priceless jewels? Perhaps the gift was too big to fit in the vault— a car, for instance. But then why wasn't it mentioned?

My connections at the State Department arranged a telephone call for me with China's President Jiang Zemin.

I confess I was quite nervous during the conversation, which took place at 3:15 p.m. EST on March 7, 2001. Here is an excerpt from the transcript:

DP: . . . uh, just seems, Mr. President that . . . um . . . the [unintelligible] . . . must have, you know . . . bestowed [unintelligible] . . . Chairman Mao, the greatest, most [unintelligible] leader China has ever known. [A long silence.] Um . . .

JZ: You are referring to the [expletive deleted] [unintelligible] *cigars!*

DP: Ohh, *no*, Mr. President, *not* Fidel Castro, sir . . . Richard Milhous *Nixon*, Mr. President . . . his—

JZ: —[EXPLETIVE DELETED] cigars! It was a *grave insult!* Not only to Chairman Mao Zedong but to *all* Chinese people. Had—[unintelligible]

DP: But . . . I don't understand. I— [connection terminated]

***

I was baffled.

How could Jiang have misunderstood? Sure, I may have mumbled a bit here and there, but the question had to have gotten through to him. In fact, I'd had to submit my questions in writing in advance. My contacts all assured me they had been delivered successfully by diplomatic pouch.

Stranger still, why would Castro's gift of the world's finest cigars be considered an insult? It made no sense.

I telephoned a source at the CIA, "Martin Burroughs," and explained the situation. Martin agreed that it was very odd and told me he'd look into it.

Three days later, an anonymous package appeared on my doorstep.

At first I was unsure whether to pick it up or call the bomb squad. My wife and I stared at it for a long moment until, finally, I screwed up my courage and told her to open it.

It contained a two-page transcript of my conversation with Jiang Zemin.

It was the complete text, with no redactions or portions labeled "unintelligible."

But that wasn't all.

Attached by paper clip was a small color photograph. Although no descriptive material accompanied the picture, I had only to glance at it and the mystery was solved.

The empty box above indicates where I'd intended to publish the photograph, along with a relevant excerpt omitted from the transcript. To my great distress, the publisher's legal department intervened and refused to allow either photo or text to appear—this despite my many protests, including a threat to abandon this book. I told them I owed it not only to my readers, but to history as well. The lawyers remained unmoved.

They never dreamed I'd publish it on the Internet at www.littleredbooks.com/thegift.htm.

Long live Chairman Mao!

A

LONG MARCH SHORTCUTS, TIPS, AND TRICKS

If you've made it this far on the Long March, you've certainly earned your rank in the People's Animation Army—maybe even a seat on the Central Committee. For your extraordinary efforts, you'll receive an official Red Guard beanie, a Chairman Mao smoking jacket (cigarettes not included), a realistic paste-on vinyl chin wart, a lifetime supply of Red Guard Deodorant, and a long list of affiliations you can use to pad your résumé. I hereby declare you a member in good standing of the Red Guard Battalion, Ground Internet Farce, Junior People's Engels Guard,[1] the Eternal AutoTween Society, Flash Art Technicians, and Proletarian Officer of the People's Strategic Tech-Art Revolution.

Just imagine how impressed future employers will be when they see this army of acronyms:

Dick (or Jane) Doe, *R.G.B.*, *G.I.F.*, *J.P.E.G.*, *E.A.T.*, *F.A.T.*, *P.O.P.S.T.A.R.*

---

[1] Informally known as the "Hell's Engels."

On the following pages you'll find a potpourri of LiveMotion tips and tricks (Macintosh commands appear in parentheses), followed by keyboard shortcuts for both the Macintosh and Windows.

To keep a scaled bitmap in your animation from looking as though it's got a bad case of pixels, be sure to use the **Make Actual Size** command on the Object menu. Select the image at the point in the animation where it's at its largest size and run the command. The image will then look its best.

You can ALT-drag (OPTION-drag) to **copy keyframes in the Timeline** (not from one object to another, however). Say you want to scale an object up and then scale it back down to its original size. Turn on the scale attribute, move the CTM, scale the object up, scale the object down, move the CTM, and then ALT-drag the first scale keyframe to where you want it.

You can **animate an object's texture** for infinite effects. Here's one quick way to make a stationary object's innards spin: Draw a shape and fill it with a texture. In the Timeline, dig down and open the object's layer1 attributes. In the Distort palette, choose Twirl, and set the Turns to 0. Advance the CTM, then click the Twirl Turns stopwatch. Advance the CTM. Adjust the distortion in the palette and advance the CTM again, and continue the process until you're sick to your stomach. Warning: Once you set out on the path of distortion, you may never return. Also, be warned that LiveMotion will generate a bitmap on every frame. To limit the number of bitmaps it generates, change the distortion keyframes to hold keyframes by right-clicking (CONTROL-clicking on a Mac) and choosing Hold. Then, by ALT-dragging (OPTION-dragging) these keyframes and entering new values on the Distort palette, you can control the number of changes made and thus the number of bitmaps generated.

Remember: **Groups have their own set of Transform attributes!** If you break apart text and group the letters, duplicate the group, and scale one of the copies, LiveMotion will export two separate groups. To make LiveMotion export just one group, turn on the scale stopwatch before scaling the group. That way LiveMotion knows that you don't want to change the size of the original artwork but you do want to scale the group that contains it.

To move an object and its motion path together, instead of adding or adjusting a position keyframe for the object, hold down CTRL-ALT (CMD-OPTION), and drag.

Here's a technique for **going full-screen** with a stand-alone Flash projector **(an .exe file only—not for use in a browser).** If you set up a link to a Flash animation using the Go to URL behavior in LiveMotion, and you want it to fill the viewer's screen, add this to the URL box: FSCommand:fullscreen. Then, in the frame popup at the bottom, type *true*.

For browsers, use a Run JavaScript behavior instead, like this:

```
var fullWin=window.open("http://www.adobe.com/products/livemotion/main.
html", "myWin", "top=0,left=0,resizable=1" + ",width=" + screen.width + ",
height=" + screen.height);
```

If you're having trouble **selecting a single object amid a cluster** (that is, if you keep accidentally selecting objects that are obscuring the one you want), select it in the Timeline list and use the four arrow keys on your keyboard (to nudge the object one frame at a time), or hold down SHIFT and use the arrow keys (to nudge it 10 frames at a time). Once you've done this, clicking on a portion of the object will select it. Or just select the object in the Timeline.

Stop ignoring **the right mouse button** (it's really a Leftist in disguise). Start right-clicking (CONTROL-clicking) on your objects, and let the magic contextual menu save you trips to the menu bar at top. This technique is also handy if you can't remember the shortcut keys.

If you're an Anti-Rightist, here's an alternate way to **transfer a LiveMotion style from one object to another:** Select the object you want to add the style to, click the Eyedropper tool, and hold down the SHIFT key. (A square will appear above the eyedropper.) Click on the object with the style. Presto!

Want to **grab a color** from another application and apply it to a vector in LiveMotion? There's no need to search for the RGB values; just snatch the color like this: Select the object you want to color, get the Eyedropper tool, and click and hold the mouse button down in an empty area of the composition. Drag the eyedropper over the color you want in the other application. Release the mouse button, and you've got it.

You can't apply LiveMotion's Photoshop filters to vectors, only to images. **To quickly change a vector into an image,** select it and press CTRL-C (CMD-C). Then paste it onto the selected object via the command Paste Special/Paste Image. You can then apply filters to the new image, though you'll no longer be able to edit its shape with the Pen and Pen Select tools.

You can create **labels on the Timeline** by adding a behavior and then naming it in the Label field of the resulting dialog box. Go to Label allows you to jump to any label you've defined in the composition, so you can navigate through the Timeline with ease.

When you use the **Load Movie behavior,** the loaded .swf file will adopt the background color of your original composition, whether you select Replace or Append. (This is not a bug, but is due to the nature of the SWF format.) To avoid this, add a texture to the composition background of the movie you want to load, or create a rectangle and fill it with the desired color; making sure it matches the composition's dimensions. When you append an .swf file, the background won't be visible and the elements of the movies loaded beneath it will show through. This technique lets you work around that behavior as well if desired.

If you add tons of Maoist treasures to **the People's Library,** LiveMotion's performance will take a hit. Try placing objects associated with different projects in their own folders within the Library (under the LiveMotion directory). That way, you can swap folders in or out as required. The Library will breathe a sigh of relief and load much quicker. This tip also works for the Styles, Textures, and Sounds palettes. You'll need to quit and relaunch LiveMotion for the changes to take effect, however.

Here's a dirty work-around for **animating the points of a path:** (1) Draw a shape. (2) Open the Object Attributes twisty in the Timeline for the object. (3) Turn on the Replace stopwatch. (4) Move the CTM to a different point in time. (5) Manually insert a keyframe by selecting the check box for the Replace attribute. (6) Move the point on the path with the Pen Selection tool. (7) Repeat steps 4 through 6. (Note: This technique doesn't create a tweened animation but rather results in a brusque shift from one value to the next.

You can **move an object's anchor point** from its default position by holding down the CTRL (CMD) key while using the Selection tool (the filled arrow) or the Subgroup Selection tool (the hollow arrow). The anchor point is the reference point for all transformations.

To reset an anchor point back to its center, choose Object •
Transform • Reset Anchor Point. Or use the Transform tool. You
can even animate the position of the anchor point by moving it and
then opening the Timeline twisty for the item's Object Attributes.

Here's something that spooked me the first time it happened by
accident. If you select an object but—mysteriously—no bounding
box appears around it, press CTRL-H (CMD-H) while the composition is active; doing so toggles the **Hide Object Edges** command in
the View menu. By the way, hiding them is helpful when you want
to quickly view a layout sans distracting edges and then turn them
on again to check for overlaps.

It's *me* again. *Thanks* for ignoring my plea for help—in the foot-
notes, *remember?* (Speed readers go to hell!) What *are* you people,
anyway?—*Commie-lovers??* Wake up! It's 2001—communism is *bank-
rupt*—it's for *losers,* for chrissakes! Or maybe you think this is a
joke—*THIS IS NO JOKE!!! THIS IS REALLY HAPPENING!!!* . . .
OK, OK, I'll calm down. . . . Look, I'm being held prisoner by the
author and his Chinese commie buddies. And right this minute
they're plotting to overthrow the U.S. government by farce. Not
laughing now, are you? I don't have much time . . . they've moved
me here to the appendix where I think they're gonna implant
some kind of device in my brain—God only knows what these god-
less bastards have planned! If they force me to look at one more
photo of Chairman Mao—I swear I'll go *STARK . . . RAVING . . .
MAD!!!* You've *got* to help me! Call the police. Call the FBI. (*Don't*
call No Starch Press—they're part of the conspiracy.) Wait!
They're coming back! I can't talk now. I'll make contact with you
somehow—on the Web!!! That's it, at www.littleredbooks.com.
Hurry, before it's too late!

Chairman Mao's Top Ten List of Long March Shortcuts

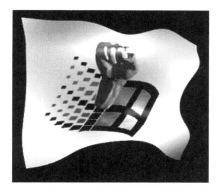 

#10. CTRL-M (Make Alias)	#10. CMD-M (Make Alias)
#9. CTRL-O^2 (Preview in Browser)	#9. CMD-O^3 (Preview in Browser)
#8. CTRL-U (Ungroup)	#8. CMD-U (Ungroup)
#7. CTRL-G (Group)	#7. CMD-G (Group)
#6. CTRL-Z (Undo)	#6. CMD-Z (Undo)
#5. CTRL-B (Paste Style)	#5. CMD-B (Paste Style)
#4. CTRL-D (Duplicate)	#4. CMD-D (Duplicate)
#3. CTRL-T (Timeline)	#3. CMD-T (Timeline)
#2. V (Selection tool)	#2. V (Selection tool)
#1. CTRL-S (Save!!!!!)	#1. CMD-S (Save!!!!!)

Most of you will have neither the time nor the inclination to memorize all (or even most) of the LiveMotion shortcuts. I offer them for only the most fanatical Red Guards who wish to score brownie points with the Central Committee's Bureau of Correct Keyboard Shortcuts. Besides, all the other books stick these charts in, so why not? That said, the Great Helmsman expects all good Revolutionaries to know his ten favorites. So if you want to please the Chairman, prepare for some self-reeducation.

---

[2] Zero.

[3] Inexplicably, Mind-CTRL-B (Brainwash) didn't make the list.

Red Chinese Takeout Reference Menu (Windows)

Tool Palette Appetizers

Crop	C
Hand	H
Eyedropper	I
Polygon	N
Subgroup Selection	A
Pen	P
Transform	E
Pen Selection	S
Type	T
Rounded Rectangle	R
Ellipse	L
Paint Bucket	K
Rectangle Tool	M
Zoom/Magnifying Glass	Z

Hot & Spicy Editing

Undo	CTRL-Z
Redo	CTRL-SHIFT-Z
Cut	CTRL-X
Copy	CTRL-C
Paste	CTRL-V
Clear	DELETE
Select All	CTRL-A
Deselect All	CTRL-SHIFT-A
Paste Style	CTRL-B
Duplicate	CTRL-D
Make Alias	CTRL-M
Break Alias	CTRL-ALT-M

Shanghai Objects

Bring to Front	CTRL-SHIFT -]
Bring Forward	CTRL -]
Send to Back	CTRL-SHIFT -[
Send Backward	CTRL-[
Apply Last Filter	CTRL-F
Make Actual Size	ALT-S

Poultry Palettes

Timeline	CTRL-T
Opacity	F5
Color	F6
Layer	F7
Properties	F8
Transform	F9
Styles	F10
Rollovers	F11
Export	CTRL-ALT-SHIFT-E
Hide All	TAB
Hide All But Tools	SHIFT-TAB

Egg Foo Views

Active Export Preview	CTRL-9
Preview Mac Gamma	CTRL-8
Preview AutoSlice	CTRL-7
Hide Object Edges	CTRL-H
Preview Motion Path	CTRL-SHIFT-Z
Zoom In	CTRL-=
Zoom Out	CTRL-HYPHEN
Actual Size	CTRL-ALT-ZERO
View Grid	CTRL-'
Snap to Grid	CTRL-SHIFT-'
View Rulers	CTRL-R
Snap to Guides	CTRL-SHIFT-;

Timeline Chow Mein

Play/Stop	SPACE BAR
Make TIG	CTRL-SHIFT-G
Next Keyframe	ALT-K
Previous Keyframe	ALT-J

* If you have the stomach for even more keyboard shortcuts, you can find them at www.adobe.com.

Red Chinese Takeout Reference Menu (Mac)

Tool Palette Appetizers

Crop	C
Hand	H
Eyedropper	I
Polygon	N
Subgroup Selection	A
Pen	P
Transform	E
Pen Selection	S
Type	T
Rounded Rectangle	R
Ellipse	L
Paint Bucket	K
Rectangle Tool	M
Zoom/Magnifying Glass	Z

Hot & Spicy Editing

Undo	CMD-Z
Redo	CMD-SHIFT -Z
Cut	CMD-X
Copy	CMD-C
Paste	CMD-V
Clear	DELETE
Select All	CMD-A
Deselect All	CMD-SHIFT-A
Paste Style	CMD-B
Duplicate	CMD-D
Make Alias	CMD-M
Break Alias	CMD-OPT-M

Shanghai Objects

Bring to Front	CMD-SHIFT -]
Bring Forward	CMD -]
Send to Back	CMD-SHIFT -[
Send Backward	CMD-[
Apply Last Filter	CMD-F
Make Actual Size	OPT-S

Poultry Palettes

Timeline	CMD-T
Opacity	F5
Color	F6
Layer	F7
Properties	F8
Transform	F9
Styles	F10
Rollovers	F11
Export	CMD-OPT-SHIFT-E
Hide All	TAB
Hide All But Tools	SHIFT-TAB

Egg Foo Views

Active Export Preview	CMD-9
Preview Mac Gamma	CMD-8
Preview AutoSlice	CMD-7
Hid Object Edges	CMD-H
Preview Motion Path	CMD-SHIFT-Z
Zoom In	CMD-=
Zoom Out	CMD-HYPHEN
Actual Size	CMD-OPT-ZERO
View Grid	CMD-'
Snap to Grid	CMD-SHIFT-'
View Rulers	CMD-R
Snap to Guides	CMD-SHIFT-;

Timeline Chow Mein

Play/Stop	SPACE BAR
Make TIG	CMD-SHIFT-G
Next Keyframe	OPT-K
Previous Keyframe	OPT-J

*If you have the stomach for even more keyboard shortcuts, you can find them at www.adobe.com.

B

MOTION RESOURCES ON THE WEB

The following links (and many more) are available in the Resources section at the book's companion Web site: www.littleredbooks.com, where they'll be updated and reeducated with fervent socialist zeal.

LiveMotion, Flash, Data, and Utilities

Adobe Systems
www.adobe.com/products/tips/livemotion.html

This is the Central Committee's compound and a source for some slick tips and tutorials, all authorized and stamped for approval by the Adobe High Command. It is your duty to check in regularly. I keep a button aimed at their mainland page on my Internet Explorer links bar and drop by every day to see what the revolutionaries are up to.

FlashJester
www.flashjester.com

No clowning around, FlashJester has some terrific utilities for customizing Flash projector files. LiveMotioneers should investigate *Woof,* which lets you search and retrieve SWF movies from your browser's cache for offline study.

FlashKiller
www.flashmagazine.com

FlashKiller was one of the first LiveMotion sites to hit the Web. It has a lively forum that explores the program from top to bottom. If you need help, stop here first. The site also has a large collection of LiveMotion templates for sale.

Flash Magazine
www.flashmagazine.com

All things Flash—news, interface experiments, and reviews.

Little Red Books
www.littleredbooks.com

For all the speed readers who might've missed this vital link.

Macromedia
www.macromedia.com

No, they're not the enemy, they're the good guys too. Without them, we'd probably be making shadows on the wall.

OpenSWF.org
www.openswf.org

The SWF format rules here. Source code and links to Third Party tools.

Stylemotion
stylemotion.com (no www)

Has a collection of .liv files, Motion tips, and resources, as well as Joe Bowden's classic preloader tutorial.

Swifty Utilities
buraks.com/swifty (no www)

Lots of *free* Flash utilities for the grabbing.

Audio and Sound Sources

Search for noise and make some.

FindSounds.com
www.findsounds.com

Music Robot
www.musicrobot.com

Whenever I need a quick f/x fix for my animations, I head for these two superb search engines. So many sounds, so little time . . .

FindSounds specializes in sound effects and lets you narrow your search by format, channel, resolution, minimum sample rate, or maximum file size

MusicRobot, of course, specializes in music—WAVs are the main course, but it also has separate engines for hunting MIDIs and even lyrics.

Free WAVs
www.thefreesite.com/Free_Sounds/Free_WAVs/index.html

An impressive collection of humorous effects—cartoon sounds, clips from movies and TV shows, and some hilarious answering machine messages as well.

Killersound
www.killersound.com

A good source for pros in need of "music and sound design for new media."

Music4flash
www.music4flash.com

A great source for loops and compilations in genre sets (vibes, urban grooves, party zone, rock). Also sound effects, button sounds, and even voices. Not free, but worth the bucks.

Font Sense

It's true. You can never have too many fonts, and now that you can show them off in your LiveMotion SWFs, there's no excuse for not stocking up. I could easily have filled 50 pages with font links, so visit the Little Red Books site for more. Note: Be sure you have a good font management tool, like Extensis Suitcase (Macintosh and Windows)—www.extensis.com; you'll need it.

BLAMBOT! Comic Fonts
www.piekosarts.com/blambotfonts

Looking for the perfect comic book font for the titles in your animated toon? BLAMBOT has the real thing for all your yows, zaps, slurrrghs, splatz, and bubbles.

The Dingbat Pages
www.dingbatpages.com

No relation to my mag, *Dingbat* (www.dingbatmag.com), this site has a vast collection of ornaments, organized alphabetically in categories like "Alien."

Erotic Fonts
www-cgrl.cs.mcgill.ca/~luc/erotic.html

Here's a precious oddity—Luc Devroye's unparalleled collection of links. You'll have to dig through some broken links, but there's plenty of gold to be found, including Chinese fonts.

The Font Diner
www.fontdiner.com

Retro, anyone?

Font World
www.fontworld.net/en/china.html

A German site featuring an archive of "Chinese look-alike" fonts. A great place to start when searching for those hard-to-find specimens.

JavaScript Resources

The JavaScript Source
javascript.internet.com (no www)

You'll find plenty of useful scripts in this ever-expanding collection. Background effects, clocks, calculators, games, forms, navigation, and more. You can sample the scripts to see how they work, copy the code from your browser, and paste it right into your page. If you're in a rush, they'll even e-mail you the script. Oh, yes, I almost forgot: the scripts are all *free.*

Web Developer's Virtual Library
www.stars.com

Where pros go into full-court code mode, feasting on PERL, CGI, XML, JavaScript, and so on.

Images

Animation Factory
www.animfactory.com

When you don't have time to do it yourself, you can choose from this collection of more than 30,000 GIFs. And you thought you were busy.

Ditto
www.ditto.com

A lot of visual search engines have disappeared recently, but Ditto and GoGraph (as of this writing) are still there to help you find just the right image.

GoGraph
www.graphsearch.com

Search for animated GIFs, photos, icons, and clip art.

The Future of Flash and Web Design

Here are some samples of Flash and Web design at its best. The future is all right here.

www.72dpi.com

www.balthaser.com

www.eye4u.com

www.eneri.net

www.sinologic.com

www.mondo.pl

www.ultrashock.com

www.shockwave.com

www.obliviance.ndirect.co.uk

Cool Art, Lit, and E-zines

I couldn't begin to describe these sites. They would require a book all their own. An avant-pop potpourri.

www.corpse.org

www.cut-here.com

www.juxtapoz.com

www.swirlpop.com

www.lemonyellow.com

www.jaguar.com/crad

www.autonomedia.com

www.cafezeitgeist.com

www.marcelduchamp.net

www.marcelduchamp.org

www.invisiblelibrary.com

www.grammatron.com/index2.html

www.whitelead.com/jrh/screenshots

www.utdallas.edu/pretext/index1a.html

www.spareroom.org/mailart/dead_check.html

entropy8zuper.org

Hardcore Maoist Mischief

See the Resources section at www.littleredbooks.com.

Little Red Bibliography

Here are some books and articles that were influential—either directly or spiritually— in the creation of this book. Every good soldier should read them.

Animation, Design, and Typography

Adobe LiveMotion f/x & Design
Daniel Gray
Coriolis (Scottsdale, AZ): 2000

I know it seems odd to plug the competition, but since Gray's book will never mistakenly wind up in the humor section, and a single book on one's favorite software is never enough, it deserves to be the next book you buy. (You owe me one, Dan.)

Alphabets & Other Signs
Edited by Julian Rothenstein and Mel Gooding
Redstone Press (London): 1991
A visual feast of forms.

Animation: 2d and Beyond
Jane Pilling
RotoVision Books (East Sussex, UK): 2001
A grand motion tome.

The Book of JavaScript: A Practical Guide to Interactive Web Pages
Thau!
No Starch Press (San Francisco): 2001
Secret code, aimed at the designer.

Color Harmony for the Web
Cailin Boyle
Rockport (Gloucester, MA): 2001
How to create sneaky color schemes.

<creative html design 2>
Lynda Weinman and William Weinman
New Riders (Indianapolis): 2001
Lynda is a know-it-all, in the very best sense.

Flash Web Design: The Art of Motion Graphics (the v5 Remix)
Hillman Curtis
New Riders (Indianapolis): 2001
Although it's specific to Macromedia Flash, the text vibes from the motion guru will enrich your LiveMotion animations.

GIF Animation Studio: Animating Your Web Site
Richard Koman
O'Reilly (Sebastopol, CA): 1996
Not a word about Flash, but a classic on the art that's still well worth reading.

Moving Type: Designing for Time and Space
Jeff Bellantoni and Matt Woolman
RotoVision Books (East Sussex, UK): 2000
Examples of cutting-edge type in time-based media.

Typology: Type Design from the Victorian Era to the Digital Age
Steven Heller and Louise Fili
Chronicle Books (San Francisco): 1999

Steve Heller is a hero, and Louise designed an early book of mine. They are the best; together they're even better.

www.color: Effective Use of Color in Web Page Design
Roger Pring
Watson-Guptill (New York): 2000

The first section is called "Seeing Red." Need I say more?

The Web Design Wow! Book
Jack Davis and Susan Merritt
Peachpit Press (Berkeley, CA): 1998

Packed with great design ideas.

Web Sites That Work
Roger Black
Adobe Press (San Jose): 1997

Theories of design that extend beyond the Web.

Chinese Politics and Magic Maoism

A Glossary of Political Terms of the People's Republic of China
Compiled by Kwok-sing Li
Chinese University Press (Hong Kong): 1995

The definitive source for navigating the maze of PRC policies and rhetoric. When you need to know the difference, say, between the "three froms and three tos" [sic] and the "three-famous and three-high," turn to this book. Reading between the lines reveals a vivid portrait of the Cultural Revolution.

The Badges of Chairman Mao Zedong
Bill Bishop
Source: www.cnd.org/CR/old/maobadge/index.html

Bishop's fascinating and detailed history of the Mao badge phenomenon is right on the button.

Chinese Propaganda Posters: From Revolution to Modernization
Stefan Landsberger
The Pepin Press (Amsterdam): 1995

A must-have for Chinese propaganda poster freaks.

Frock Purge
Edited by Liu Shao-Chi, Lin Chu Pel, and Teng Wensheng
Not Guilty Press (Vineyard Haven, MA): 1969

A mimeographed oddity that sparked my fascination with Mao.

Mao: A Life
Philip Short
Henry Holt & Company (New York): 1999

A beautifully written biography.

The Private Life of Chairman Mao
Dr. Li Zhisui
Random House (New York): 1994

A portrait of the Great Helmsman as Grand Philanderer.

Red Guards: Hong Wei Bing
Revolutionary Worker #966: July 19, 1998

A glamorized account of the Red Guard movement. Ah, those crazy kids.

Revolutionary Rudeness: The Language of Red Guards and
Rebel Workers in China's Cultural Revolution
Elizabeth J. Perry and Li Xun
University of California, Berkeley: 1993 (Thesis)

As the VP would say, we're talking rude—big time.

Songs of the Red Guards: Keywords Set to Music
Vivian Wagner
University of Heidelberg: n.d. (Thesis)

The author analyzes all of the catchy lyrics from those unforgettable Red Guard standards.

Absurdism, Humor, and Quality Lit

The Complete Nonsense of Edward Lear
Edited by Holbrook Jackson
Dover Publications (New York): 1951

Utter nonsense.
> *"There was an old Chairman from China/*
> *Whose writings (decidedly mynah)/*
> *Set roosters astirring and running-dogs scurrying/*
> *That feisty old Chairman from China!"*

Exercises in Style
Raymond Queneau
New Directions (New York): 1979

One pedestrian incident told in 99 different styles.

On Semantic Poetry
Stefan Themerson
Gaberbocchus Press (London): 1975

"I would rather feel it than be able to define it."

Oulipo: A Primer of Potential Literature
Warren K. Motte Jr.
University of Nebraska Press (Lincoln): 1986

An absurdist bible for experimental writers.

The Selected Works of Alfred Jarry
Edited by Roger Shattuck and Simon Watson Taylor
Grove Press (New York): 1965

Patron Saint of the Absurd. Had Jarry lived to see the Chairman, his classic play Ubu Roi would have been a revolutionary model opera.

The Wonderful World of Alphonse Allais
Translated by Miles Kington
Chatto & Windus (London): 1977

A literary sprinter. Although he comes in last here, he still manages to win the race.[1] Allais is one of the funniest writers that ever lived.

---

[1] He deserves (and would surely have appreciated) this athlete's footnote.

Some Other Books by Derek Pell And Norman Conquest, Too

Advantages of Being a Saint
The Invention of Style
Frozen Sunlight
Scar Mirror
Expurgations
Endangered Beasties
The Suicide Guidebook
Brother Spencer Goes to Hell
This Oswald Himself Was Not
The Marquis de Sade's Elements of Style
True Tiny Tales of Terror (with Ann Hodgman)
Doktor Bey's Handbook of Strange Sex
Doktor Bey's Bedside Bug Book
Doktor Bey's Book of Brats
Doktor Bey's Book of the Dead
Morbid Curiosities
Assassination Rhapsody
X-Texts
As Norman Conquest
Interiors: A Book of Very Clean Rooms
A Beginner's Guide to Art Deconstruction
By Any Means: An Avant-Pop Anthology
Eight Adult Males & Other Odd Tales
Selected Poems of Edward D. Wood, Jr.
Straight Razor (with Harold Jaffe)
Sartre's French Phrase Book

INDEX

Add Behavior • Stop, 95

preloader options, 164

targeting a frame in, *174*

URL list box, *155*

Edit menu

Composition Settings, 18, 19, 119

Make Alias, 48

Paste Object Animation, 72

Paste Style, 91

Preferences, 18, 27

Edit mode, switching from Preview
mode to, 45

Edit mode button, 18

keyboard shortcut for, 90

Edit Original command, 100

eliseblack.com, 102

Ellipse tool, *27*

Outline, 21, 27, 69

Properties tab, 27

using to draw a circle, 48

End behavior, 161

Entire Composition, 19

error messages during file exports,
119

events. *See* behaviors

Event Sound, 142

Exclude, 34

Expand/Collapse control, 58

Export palette, 112–113

Indexed, 145

using with sound files, *152*–153

export reports, 110–112

Export Settings, 88

eyeball icons, 47

Eyedropper tool, 27

F

fade-outs, sound, 150–*152*

File menu

Export, 146

Export Settings, 88

New, 18

Place, 99

Preview In, 79

files. *See also* animated GIFs; bitmaps;
HTML files; sound files

backing up, 11

exporting, 110–113

format options for exported, 112

importing, 99–106

importing sequences of images,
106–107

.liv, 11

MP3, 140

naming of, 106

organizing, 11

preserving LiveMotion original, 11

reducing the size of, 107–113,
129–130, 154, 187

.swf, 1

working simultaneously with
multiple, 172

Fill, 17

Filters, 100

F6 (keyboard shortcut), 88

F11 (keyboard shortcut), 89

Flash

"frameline" (Timeline), 1, 18, 54

strengths, 125n1

weaknesses, 1, 19, 54

Flash animations. *See* animations

Flash files

exporting sound to, *152*–153

generating for export, 146

(.swf) format, 1

Flip Horizontal, 91

font. *See* type

Four-way Blend, 47

Frame drop-down menu, *174*, 175

freeware to use with LiveMotion,

12–13

G

GoLive, 13

Go to URL behavior

on Add Behavior menu, *92*

adding to rollover buttons, 174

URL list box, 155

using at end of animations, 188

gradient fills, 27

graphics examples

abstract art, *25*

button, 28

Chicken man, *26*

Chinese character, 20–24

red square with black outline, 17

red star, 24–25

Group, 119

grouped objects. *See* objects in groups

guide lines, *75*–76

H

handles, in bounding boxes, 23

heart with kissing silhouettes

(animation example), 94–96

Horizontal Centers, 30, 89

HTML files

exporting objects and layouts to,

118–119, 174–175

loading, with JavaScript, 183

naming of, 183

replacing text in, with graphic

buttons, 119–*121*

I

Ignore Color of First Layer, 48

Illustrator

layered files, importing into

LiveMotion, 99

shortcut to, 100

using with LiveMotion, 12

images

copying, 88

creating layered, 99

sequential, 106–107

Images folder, 118

ImageStyler, 1, *2*

Indexed (file format), 145

Insert Sound button, 141

interactivity in animations, 64

Intersect, 34

Invert, 177

J

JavaScript

adding custom commands, 92

browser variations in displaying, 182

code for opening a new window, 183

created by LiveMotion, 118

running, in LiveMotion, 183–*184*

JPEG files, changing to Indexed format, 145

K

keyboard shortcuts. See also mouse and keyboard shortcuts; mouse shortcuts; shortcuts

complete list of, 199, 200–201

to display Timeline, 46

to duplicate an image, 17

for making multiple copies, 172

for pasting, 132

for Preview mode, 90

to reveal Color palette, 88

to reveal Rollover palette, 89

to select all objects, 132

to select the Type tool, 49

to select tools, 18

signaling that a download is complete, 165

for switching between Pen and Pen Selection tools, 22

for undo, 22

keyframes, 54–55

adding, in Timeline, *117*

copying, 61–62

definition of, 54n2

Ease Out transitions, 65

staggered, *72*

in a Timeline, *133*

Timeline icons for, 56–67

working with, 58–59

kiss animation, creating, 95–96

L

Lasso tool (Adobe Photoshop), 101

Layer, 58

Layer Offset tool, 16

keyboard shortcut for, 18

layers, 44

adding to vector objects, 108

using in animations, 101–102, *103*

working with, in Photoshop, 100, *102*

layers-turned-objects, 99, *103*, 114, *115*

layout examples

Flash-based "Manchurian Candidate," 175–184

Web home page, *118*

layouts. *See also* compositions

backgrounds in, 51, 188, *189*

comparing two, *172*

designing, 170–174

exporting to HTML, 118–119, 174–175

sketching out rough drafts of, 10–*11*

sliced, 119

specifying grid spacing for, 27

uses for, on the Web, 184–188

SoundForge, *(continued)*

version 4.5, 185

Sound icon, 147

Sound library, 141

location of, 147

sound objects

adding to rollover buttons, 146–148

adjusting, *142*, 143

compared with sound effects, 147

compression rates for, 152–153

continuous looping of, 143, 144

continuous looping of a group of, 149–150

duration bars for, 141

extending the length of, 143

fading out, 150–*152*

making TIGs with, 149–150

naming or renaming of, 142

sounds

converting stereo into mono, 153

exporting to Flash files, *152*–153

why use in animations, 156

Sounds palette, *140*–141

special effects, 28. *See also* sound effects

splash screens, creating, 186–188

Start behavior, 161

states, 89

attaching rollover buttons to, 177

attaching sounds to, 146–147

Stop behavior, 95, 97

stopwatch icon, 58

stormy weather (animation example), 60–62

streaming sound, 140

style layers, viewing, 47

styles

adding to text, 129

copying and pasting, 49–50

customizing of, 47–49

definition of, 44

using, 47

Styles palette, 44–45

icons, *45*

selecting Preview mode in, 47

Subgroup Selection tool, 16, *32*–33

Swatches view, 42

.swf file format, 1

SWfx, 13

Swish, 13

T

text. *See also* type

adding styles to, 129

repositioning and manipulating, 70

transforming into bitmap images, 80

text animation examples

an anagram, 82, *83*

Mao in Motion, 73–78

six red anagrams, 70–72

text animations, 68

basic steps in creating, 78

estimating the size of, 79

keyboard shortcut for saving, 76

making changes to, without tweening, 80

setting the length of, 76

tweening, *(continued)*

    when to avoid, 81

twisties (triangle-shaped icons), 58

type. *See also* text

    audience created from, 184–*185*

    bold, 74

    colors of, 69

    exporting from LiveMotion, 79

    styles for, 74

Type tool, 49, 68–70, 74, 75

    dialog box, *69*

    strengths and weaknesses, 17–18

U

Uncombine command, 35

undo, 22

Ungroup command, 35

Unite, 33, *34*

Unite with Color, 33, *34*, 177

Until, 164

URL text entry box, *155*. *See also* Go
    to URL behavior

V

vector objects

    adding layers to, 108

    compared with bitmaps, 109

    switching to bitmaps from,
        186–187

vertical lines in object duration bars,
    151

View Big Textures button, 50

View menu, 27

    Active Export Preview, 109

    Show Rulers, 75–76

View Small Textures button, 50

visual effects, creating, 28

V (keyboard shortcut), 18

Volume attribute, 142

Volume slider bar, 151, *152*

W

Wait for Download behavior, 161

    effect on animation previews, 165

"Waiting for Godot" (preloader
    example), *161*–165

"Wao Mao" (animation example),
    78–80

Web Adaptive, 145

Web buttons. *See* rollover buttons

Web palette, 119, *120*

Web site building

    home page examples, *118*,
        175–184

    planning layouts for, 170–173

    using LiveMotion for, 169

    See also layouts

Web site companion to this book.
    See littleredbooks.com

Web sites of interest

    dingbatmag.com, 187

    eliseblack.com, 102

    Shockwave.com, 160

Web zines, creating, 185–186

White Bone Demon symbol, 6

STEAL THIS COMPUTER BOOK 2
What They Won't Tell You About the Internet

by WALLACE WANG

The same informative, irreverent, and entertaining style that made the first edition a huge success discusses Internet security issues like viruses, cracking, and password theft. Also covered are Trojan horse programs, illegal copying of MP3 files, computer forensics, and encryption. A new CD-ROM contains hundreds of anti-hacker and security tools.

2000, 400 PP. W/CD-ROM, $24.95 ($37.95 CDN)
ISBN 1-886411-42-5

THE OPERA 5.x BOOK
Browsing the Web with Speed and Style

by J.S. LYSTER

Learn to take full advantage of this fast, powerful, and free Web browser's features, including how to retrieve multiple documents simultaneously and navigate entirely with the keyboard. CD-ROM includes trial versions of Opera 5.x for all platforms, as well as other utilities and plug-ins.

2001, 336 PP. W/CD-ROM, $29.95 ($44.95 CDN)
ISBN 1-886411-47-6

THE BOOK OF JAVASCRIPT
A Practical Guide to Interactive Web Pages

by THAU!

Rather than offer cut-and-paste solutions, this tutorial/reference focuses on understanding JavaScript, and shows Web designers how to customize and implement JavaScript on their sites. The CD-ROM includes code for each example in the book, script libraries, and relevant software.

2000, 424 PP. W/CD-ROM, $29.95 ($44.95 CDN)
ISBN 1-886411-36-0

THE BLENDER BOOK
Free 3D Graphics Software for the Web and Video

by CARSTEN WARTMANN

The Blender Book's step-by-step tutorials demystify its complex interface and show how to enhance and animate Web sites, graphic designs, and video productions; use materials and textures; work with skeleton animation and kinematics; and integrate 3D objects into videos.

2001, 350 PP. W/CD-ROM, $39.95 ($59.95 CDN)
ISBN 1-886411-44-1

JOE NAGATA'S LEGO MINDSTORMS IDEA BOOK

by JOE NAGATA

Joe Nagata's LEGO MINDSTORMS Idea Book shows readers how to build 10 exciting robots using LEGO MINDSTORMS, with ideas for building many more. Over 250 step-by-step illustrations make these projects easy for users at all levels.

2001, 184 PP., $21.95 ($32.95 CDN)
ISBN 1-886411-40-9

Phone:

1 (800) 420-7240 OR
(415) 863-9900
MONDAY THROUGH FRIDAY,
9 A.M. TO 5 P.M. (PST)

Fax:

(415) 863-9950
24 HOURS A DAY,
7 DAYS A WEEK

Email:

SALES@NOSTARCH.COM

Web:

HTTP://WWW.NOSTARCH.COM

Mail:

NO STARCH PRESS
555 DE HARO STREET, SUITE 250
SAN FRANCISCO, CA 94107
USA

Distributed in the U.S. by Publishers Group West

UPDATES

The book was carefully reviewed for technical accuracy, but it's inevitable that some things will change after the book goes to press. Visit the Web site for this book at **http://www.littleredbooks.com** for updates, errata, and other information.